W9-DGE-927

To

_____

From

_____

Date

_____

*100 Days of Grace & Gratitude: A Devotional Journal*
© 2018 DaySpring Cards, Inc. All rights reserved.
Artwork © 2018 Shanna Noel. Used by permission.
First Edition, September 2018

Published by:

P.O. Box 1010
Siloam Springs, AR 72761
dayspring.com

All rights reserved. *100 Days of Grace & Gratitude: A Devotional Journal* is under copyright protection. No part of this book may be used or reproduced in any manner whatsoever without written permission except in the case of brief quotations embodied in critical articles and reviews.

Unless otherwise noted, Scripture is taken from the Holman Christian Standard Bible®. Copyright © 1999, 2000, 2002, 2003, 2009 by Holman Bible Publishers. Used by permission. HCSB® is a federally registered trademark of Holman Bible Publishers.

Scripture quotations marked NET are taken from NET Bible® copyright ©1996–2006 by Biblical Studies Press, L.L.C. http://netbible.com All rights reserved.

Scripture quotations marked NIV are taken from THE HOLY BIBLE, NEW INTERNATIONAL VERSION®, NIV® Copyright © 1973, 1978, 1984, 2011 by Biblica, Inc.® Used by permission. All rights reserved worldwide.

Scripture quotations marked TLB are taken from The Living Bible copyright © 1971 by Tyndale House Foundation. Used by permission of Tyndale House Publishers Inc., Carol Stream, Illinois 60188. All rights reserved. The Living Bible, TLB, and the The Living Bible logo are registered trademarks of Tyndale House Publishers.

Scripture quotations marked ESV are taken from The ESV® Bible (The Holy Bible, English Standard Version®). ESV® Text Edition: 2016. Copyright © 2001 by Crossway, a publishing ministry of Good News Publishers. The ESV text has been reproduced in cooperation with and by permission of Good News Publishers. Unauthorized reproduction of this publication is prohibited. All rights reserved.

Scripture quotations marked AMP are taken from the Amplified Bible. Copyright © 2015 by The Lockman Foundation, La Habra, CA 90631. All rights reserved.

Scripture quotations marked NLT are taken from *Holy Bible*, New Living Translation, copyright © 1996, 2004, 2015 by Tyndale House Foundation. Used by permission of Tyndale House Publishers, Inc., Carol Stream, Illinois 60188. All rights reserved.

Scripture quotations marked CSB are taken from the Christian Standard Bible. Copyright © 2017 by Holman Bible Publishers. Used by permission. Christian Standard Bible®, and CSB® are federally registered trademarks of Holman Bible Publishers, all rights reserved.

Scripture quotations marked CEV are taken from the Contemporary English Version® Copyright © 1995 American Bible Society. All rights reserved.

Scripture quotations marked CEB are taken from the Common English Bible. © Copyright 2011 by the Common English Bible. All rights reserved. Used by permission.

Scripture quotations marked NLV are taken from the New Life Version copyright © 1969 and 2003. Used by permission of Barbour Publishing, Inc., Uhrichsville, Ohio, 44683. All rights reserved.

Scripture quotations marked NASB are taken from the NEW AMERICAN STANDARD BIBLE®, Copyright © 1960, 1962, 1963, 1968, 1971, 1972, 1973, 1975, 1977, 1995 by The Lockman Foundation. Used by permission.

Scripture quotations marked GW are taken from GOD'S WORD®, © 1995 God's Word to the Nations. Used by permission of Baker Publishing Group.

Scripture quotations marked GNT are taken from the Good News Translation® (Today's English Version, Second Edition) Copyright © 1992 American Bible Society. All rights reserved.

Scripture quotations marked ICB are taken from the International Children's Bible® Copyright© 2015 by Tommy Nelson, a division of Thomas Nelson, Inc.

Scripture quotations marked NIRV are taken from the New International Reader's Version. Copyright © 1995, 1996, 1998, 2014 by Biblica, Inc.®. Used by permission. All rights reserved worldwide.

Scripture quotations marked THE MESSAGE are taken from *The Message*. Copyright © 1993, 1994, 1995, 1996, 2000, 2001, 2002. Used by permission of NavPress Publishing Group.

Scripture quotations marked NKJV are taken from the New King James Version®. Copyright © 1982 by Thomas Nelson. Used by permission. All rights reserved.

Scripture quotations marked RSV are taken from the Revised Standard Version of the Bible, copyright © 1946, 1952, and 1971 the Division of Christian Education of the National Council of the Churches of Christ in the United States of America. Used by permission. All rights reserved.

Scripture quotations marked VOICE are taken from The Voice Bible Copyright © 2012 Thomas Nelson, Inc. The Voice™ translation © 2012 Ecclesia Bible Society All rights reserved.

Typeset Design by Jessica Wei

Printed in China.

Prime: 10983
ISBN: 978-1-68408-570-5

# — 100 DAYS OF —
# Grace & gratitude

## A Devotional Journal

## SHANNA NOEL

### WITH LISA STILWELL

# IT'S A NEW DAY

Today is a brand-new day that God has made just for you. It's a day that's bright and fresh, ready and waiting for new beginnings to unfold. No matter what happened yesterday, today is new. That means new thoughts, new prayers, new worship, new hope, and new chances to recognize and rejoice in God's goodness. Yesterday is behind you; tomorrow is out of reach. Today is an unexplored treasure with adventures waiting. May your heart be full of grace and peace as you embrace this promising new start in front of you.

Take off your former way of life, the old self . . .
to be renewed in the spirit of your minds.
Ephesians 4:22-23 CSB

Sing a new song to the LORD;
sing His praise from the ends of the earth.
Isaiah 42:10

Do not conform to the pattern of this world,
but be transformed by the renewing of your mind.
Then you will be able to test and approve what God's will is—
His good, pleasing and perfect will.
Romans 12:2 NIV

This is the day the LORD has made.
We will rejoice and be glad in it.
Psalm 118:24 NLT

PRAYER:

Lord, thank You for this bright, new day. I rejoice
that I get to walk and work each moment in the safety
of Your presence and the joy of Your love.

# HIS GIFTS ARE PERFECT

Have you ever received a gift and thought, *Wow, what a great gift—it's perfect!* Thinking back, why was it so wonderful? Perhaps because only someone who knew you really well could have made it so personal. And because that person took the time and consideration to give something he or she knew would mean a lot to you. That is how thoughtful and loving our God is. He knows you better than anyone. His gifts of peace, mercy, and forgiveness are carefully measured and given at just the right times, in the most perfect ways you need. His care for you is endless. His love for you gets poured out through His grace and righteousness in the very details of your life. He is good.

Now grace was given to each one of us according
to the measure of the Messiah's gift.
Ephesians 4:7

If you then, who are evil, know how to give good gifts
to your children, how much more will your Father in
heaven give good things to those who ask Him!
Matthew 7:11

See, the Lord God comes with strength,
and His power establishes His rule.
His reward is with Him, and His gifts accompany Him.
Isaiah 40:10

Whatever is good and perfect comes to
us from God, the Creator of all light.

James 1:17 TLB

**PRAYER:**

Father, not a day passes that I don't receive gifts from
You in just the ways I need. May I see them as Your "I
love you's" chosen and given specifically for me, to
bless my heart and to remind me of Your presence.

# THE FULLNESS
# OF HIS GRACE

When you're in the midst of a struggle—whether tragedy, sickness, betrayal, or hardship—human nature wants to look at the problem and do what's natural: worry, fret, or get even. But God gives another option: trust in Him. When you do, you will receive His peace—His perfect peace for the very moment you're in. He knows all that you're facing, and, even with chaos ensuing on the outside, you can walk in the fullness of His grace and peace on the inside. What will you trust Him with today?

I will both lie down and sleep in peace,
for You alone, Lord, make me live in safety.
Psalm 4:8

Since we have been declared righteous by faith,
we have peace with God through our Lord Jesus Christ.
Romans 5:1

The Lord gives strength to His people;
the Lord blesses His people with peace.
Psalm 29:11 NIV

He will keep in perfect peace all those who trust
in Him, whose thoughts turn often to the Lord!

Isaiah 26:3 TLB

## PRAYER:

Father, thank You for Your promise to bless me with Your
true and lasting peace, no matter what I'm facing.

# WHAT DO YOU THINK ABOUT?

Did you know that your mind literally expands on whatever you focus on? If you focus on what you're afraid of, your mind expands with fear and gloom. If you think about what you're grateful for, your mind expands with optimism and contentment. So if you start your day with negative thoughts, stop! Make a conscious decision to take those thoughts captive and think on whatever is true and pure and lovely. After you do, the feelings will follow, and before you know it, peace will rule your day.

I have asked one thing from the LORD; it is what I desire:
to dwell in the house of the LORD all the days of my life,
gazing on the beauty of the LORD and seeking Him in His temple.
Psalm 27:4

I stay awake through the night
to think about Your promises.
Psalm 119:148 TLB

I pray that He may grant you,
according to the riches of His glory,
to be strengthened with power in the inner man
through His Spirit, and that the Messiah
may dwell in your hearts through faith.
Ephesians 3:16-17

Finally [sisters], whatever is true, whatever is honorable, whatever is just, whatever is pure, whatever is lovely, whatever is commendable—if there is any moral excellence and if there is any praise—dwell on these things.

Philippians 4:8

## PRAYER:

Oh, Lord, please help me take my thoughts captive to nothing but Your goodness and mercy in my life. I love You and want to walk in a spirit of joy no matter what I face today.

# WALKING WITH JOY

Have you ever thought that, while Jesus walked the earth, He walked with His Father's joy? Yes, while casting out demons, healing the sick, walking, and preaching to the point of exhaustion, Jesus was joy-filled. And before He left the earth, He said that when you remain in Him and live out His purpose for your life, you can have His joy too. In fact, His joy is made complete in you. This means that no matter what work or challenges you face, you can accomplish and overcome each with His joy to the fullest.

The hope of the righteous is joy.
Proverbs 10:28

For to the man who is pleasing in His sight,
He gives wisdom, knowledge, and joy.
Ecclesiastes 2:26

You lead me in the path of life;
I experience absolute joy in Your presence;
You always give me sheer delight.
Psalm 16:11 NET

If you obey My commandments,
you will remain in My love, just as I have obeyed
My Father's commandments and remain in His love.
I have told you these things so that My joy
`may be in you, and your joy may be complete.

John 15:10-11 NET

**PRAYER:**

Father, thank You for Your gifts of wonder and delight.
Fill my heart and mind, hold me and protect me as I walk
in the fullness of Your joy throughout this day.

# NOTHING IS TOO SMALL

Each new day is filled with things to be thankful for—from big events such as having another day of life, to small ones such as finding matching socks in the dryer (although sometimes that can seem big!). But in our busyness and struggles, it's easy to forget to give thanks. Sometimes our feelings don't lend to thoughts of gratefulness—it's much easier to dwell on what is wrong rather than what is right. When that happens, the best cure is to start giving thanks about anything—the key is just to start. Give thanks for the first thing that comes to mind—nothing is too small. All gratefulness builds into a big deposit of love for the One who gives us reason to live and praise His name.

I . . . go around Your altar, LORD,
raising my voice in thanksgiving
and telling about Your wonderful works.
Psalm 26:6-7

I'm grateful to God.
II Timothy 1:3 CEB

Praise the LORD!
Oh give thanks to the LORD,
for He is good,
for His steadfast love endures forever!
Psalm 106:1 ESV

# day 6

Let the message about the Messiah
dwell richly among you, teaching and
admonishing one another in all wisdom,
and singing psalms, hymns, and spiritual songs,
with gratitude in your hearts to God.

Colossians 3:16

## PRAYER

Father, thank You for loving me, for providing for my
needs, for being with me wherever I go, and for helping
me throughout each day. Thank You for shoes to wear, hot
water to bathe in, and food to eat. You are so generous
and giving in countless ways, and I am grateful.

# GRACE IS...

Grace is overlooking an offense. It is not seeking payback toward someone who's wronged you. It's covering someone else's shortcomings with quiet love. It is paying someone else's debt for nothing in return. Grace is stepping into someone else's place when they aren't able to be there. Grace is . . . Jesus taking on our sin before we ever even loved Him. Grace is what God extends to us each and every day.

It seems there are no words to express enough gratitude to equal the gift of grace, yet gratefulness is the best response. So begin today, and every day, with thanksgiving and gladness for God's grace.

All creation, come praise the name of the Lord.
Praise His name alone.
The glory of God is greater than heaven and earth.
Psalm 148:13 CEV

Now I [Paul] commit you to God and
to the message of His grace,
which is able to build you up and to give you
an inheritance among all who are sanctified.
Acts 20:32

But God proves His own love for us
in that while we were still sinners, Christ died for us!
Romans 5:8

day

7

Where sin multiplied,
grace multiplied even more.
Romans 5:20

PRAYER:

Father, my life would be so broken and lost, even
devastating, without Your grace covering my sin, my
shortcomings, my faults, mistakes. Thank You from the
depths of my heart for covering me with such a gift.

# HUMILITY BEFORE GRACE

Humility and grace go hand in hand. It takes humility to admit you are a sinner, and grace to lift your head from shame. When humility knocks for God, grace opens the door. Humility empties the heart of dirt, and grace fills it up with holiness and blessing. Humility puts others first, grace overlooks on days you forget. Humility and grace are like conjoined twins—one can't survive without the other. So if you're looking for grace, call on humility, and grace won't be far behind.

God resists the proud,
but gives grace to the humble.
James 4:6

Humble yourselves before the Lord,
and He will lift you up.
James 4:10 NIV

Do nothing out of rivalry or conceit,
but in humility consider others
as more important than yourselves.
Philippians 2:3

He adorns the humble with salvation.
Psalm 149:4

All of you clothe yourselves
with humility toward one another,
because God resists
the proud but gives grace to the humble.

I Peter 5:5

**PRAYER:**

Lord, humbling myself is sometimes a moment-by-moment thing—
pride keeps knocking. But I humble myself now.
I want to see the full extent of Your grace in my life.

# HIS GRACE
# IN FORGIVENESS

No one is immune—we are all susceptible to that flash of anger when someone's been rude, disrespectful, or even mean. When that happens, we can spend an entire day, even an entire lifetime, holding onto the pain and offense. We continue thinking about how we'd like to lash back and get even. But Jesus calls us to a different response, and that is . . . forgiveness. It's such a beautiful word, until we're the one having to extend it. But forgiveness is vital for living in the freedom Christ intended. It's why He died for us on the cross. We all need forgiveness—God's and one another's—in order to fully know the meaning of grace.

How joyful is the one whose transgression is forgiven,
whose sin is covered!
Psalm 32:1

But the free gift of Christ isn't like Adam's failure.
If many people died through what one person did wrong,
God's grace is multiplied even more for many people
with the gift—of the one person Jesus Christ—
that comes through grace.
Romans 5:15 CEB

And be kind and compassionate to one another,
forgiving one another, just as God also forgave you in Christ.
Ephesians 4:32

day **9**

Forgive us the wrongs we have done,
as we forgive the wrongs
that others have done to us.
Matthew 6:12 GNT

Oh, Father, please forgive me for harboring unforgiveness toward
_____ . I need Your help. It's not easy. But by Your grace,
power, and love, I humble myself and ask that You help me to forgive.

# SAVED BY GRACE

From the time we're born, we are conditioned by cause and effect. If we do something good, we are recognized and praised. If we make a mistake, we are judged and held accountable until it's made right. We cause our actions to effect reward, acceptance, and restitution. This is why it's so hard for many to grasp the concept of grace. Out of His mercy, Christ died for us in order to remove man-made conditions so that we could live free under God's grace. The ultimate cause of Jesus's death effected freedom and grace in our lives. We no longer have to "do" anything except believe it and accept it. Have you?

> Together with Christ Jesus He also raised us up and
> seated us in the heavens, so that in the coming ages
> He might display the immeasurable riches of His grace
> through His kindness to us in Christ Jesus.
> Ephesians 2:6–7

> He saved us, not because of the righteous things we had done,
> but because of His mercy. He washed away our sins,
> giving us a new birth and new life through the Holy Spirit.
> Titus 3:5 NLT

> For we have all received from His fullness
> one gracious gift after another.
> For the law was given through Moses,
> but grace and truth came about through Jesus Christ.
> John 1:16–17 NET

For you are saved by grace through faith,
and this is not from yourselves;
it is God's gift—not from works,
so that no one can boast.
Ephesians 2:8-9

## PRAYER:

Father, thank You for the sacrifice of Your Son so that I
can live in the covenant of Your grace. Now help me to fully
embrace it and walk in the freedom that is now mine.

# GRUMBLE OR GRATEFUL?

Grumbling and gratitude simply don't mix. While every minute of every day presents opportunities to do both, they can't be done at the same time. It's either/or, and there's always a choice. The thing is, when you express thanks and gratitude to someone, God hears. And when you grumble to someone, God hears. They each set a precedent for how you are actually approaching God deep within your heart— not to mention the testimony on display for people who are watching. Grateful or grumble—which will it be?

Be thankful. Let the message of Christ dwell among you richly as you teach and admonish one another with all wisdom through psalms, hymns, and songs from the Spirit, singing to God with gratitude in your hearts.
Colossians 3:15-16 NIV

These people are discontented grumblers,
walking according to their desires;
their mouths utter arrogant words,
flattering people for their own advantage.
Jude 16

I will hope continually and will praise You more and more.
My mouth will tell about Your righteousness
and Your salvation all day long.
Psalm 71:14-15

## day 11

You are not grumbling against us,
but against the LORD.

Exodus 16:8 NIV

### PRAYER:

Father, please forgive my grumbling—I know it affects my
mood, my faith, and my testimony. Thank You for fresh, new
beginnings for turning my complaints into praise for You.

# THANKSGIVING AND PRAISE... EVERY DAY

If you were to stop and thank God for anything right now, what would it be? In fact, do just that—stop and give thanks for whatever comes to mind. Is it the ability to take another breath? Having eyes to see His creation? Tasting a fresh-picked strawberry? Getting a big hug from a loved one? If you think about it, you could write a list of things to be thankful for literally every day for the rest of your life—His goodness is endless. To focus on His greatness even a small amount is enough to spark an attitude of praise into a full-blown fire of His joy unceasing. What will be on your list today?

I will give You thanks with all my heart;
I will sing Your praise before the heavenly beings.
I will bow down toward Your holy temple and give thanks
to Your name for Your constant love and truth.
Psalm 138:1-2

Yahweh, You are my God; I will exalt You.
I will praise Your name, for You have accomplished wonders,
plans formed long ago, with perfect faithfulness.
Isaiah 25:1

And Mary said, "My soul magnifies the Lord,
and my spirit rejoices in God my Savior."
Luke 1:46-47 ESV

Every day I will thank You;
I will praise You forever and ever.
The LORD is great and is to be highly praised;
His greatness is beyond understanding.

Psalm 145:2-3 GNT

PRAYER:

Father, You are so good and so great.
Thank You for Your endless supply of blessings,
even the ones that are yet to come.
I love You and praise Your holy name.

# PRAISE HIS HOLY NAME

If you are struggling to find reason to praise God, these verses offer powerful ideas to get your heart and mind started. Thinking on the beauty of the heavens, remembering His powerful acts, recalling the abundance He has graced your life with ample cause to rejoice and be glad. Don't let the enemy have your focus and pull you into defeat. Let everything that breathes—including you—praise the Lord today.

Be exalted, Lord, in Your strength;
we will sing and praise Your might.
Psalm 21:13

Praise the Lord, the God of Israel,
because He has visited
and provided redemption for His people.
Luke 1:68

Rejoice, you Gentiles, with His people! And again:
Praise the Lord, all you Gentiles;
all the peoples should praise Him!
Romans 15:10-11

day 13

Hallelujah!
Praise God in His sanctuary.
Praise Him in His mighty heavens.
Praise Him for His powerful acts;
praise Him for His abundant greatness. . . .
Let everything that breathes praise the LORD.
Hallelujah!

Psalm 150:1-2, 6

PRAYER:

Father, I ascribe to You the glory due Your name and worship You in the splendor of Your holiness. You are great and mighty, and I am thankful to be Your child.

# PRAISE HIM
# IN THE NIGHT

Waking up at 2 a.m. and chasing a mind that won't stop running is exhausting. The enemy loves nothing more than to rob your joy, your peace, your hope, and your sleep. But almighty God is ever-present. At the call of His name, He is there to console, instruct, guide, and most of all, make the enemy flee. Praise the One who helps and counsels at all times—even in the wee hours of the morning. He loves you and is with you. Just call on His name.

Hold on to instruction; don't let go.
Guard it, for it is your life.
Proverbs 4:13

"Sacrifice thank offerings to God,
fulfill your vows to the Most High,
and call on Me in the day of trouble;
I will deliver you, and you will honor Me."
Psalm 50:14-15 NIV

Give thanks to the LORD!
Call on His name!
Psalm 105:1 NET

I will praise the LORD who counsels me—
even at night my conscience instructs me.
Psalm 16:7

## PRAYER:

Lord God, thank You for being
at my beck and call no matter the hour.
I'm so grateful You don't leave me wondering
what to do about my life—
You are with me, leading and guiding,
even when I don't realize it.

# TRUST IS KEY

Stepping outside to face the day and its demands can often feel as though you're walking into a battlefield. That's because you are! God says we will have trouble and hardships both big and small. But He doesn't leave us to face them alone. When you trust in Him, no matter what happens, He promises to strengthen and shield you from the elements of harm. He's your personal guard watching and protecting you at all times. Knowing this—and really believing it—is enough to rest in Him and put a song in your heart today, no matter what you're about to face.

You are my hiding place from every storm of life;
You even keep me from getting into trouble!
You surround me with songs of victory.
Psalm 32:7 TLB

Let the message about the Messiah
dwell richly among you . . . singing psalms,
hymns, and spiritual songs,
with gratitude in your hearts to God.
Colossians 3:16

I have told you these things so that in Me you may have peace.
You will have suffering in this world.
Be courageous! I have conquered the world.
John 16:33

The LORD is my strength and my shield;
my heart trusts in Him, and I am helped.
Therefore my heart rejoices,
and I praise Him with my song.

Psalm 28:7

## PRAYER:

Father, thank You for Your strength,
because I don't have any. And thank You for
Your protection, because I need it.
My heart sings with praise for You
and how You care for me each day.

# WHAT DO YOU SEE?

God's love is before your very eyes. Really, it's all around. No matter where you are, take a look and start counting His touches of love. If you're inside, there are walls holding a roof over your head. Electricity and a place to sit and rest are part of His provision. If you're outside, you have the warmth of the sun, birds chirping, and a soft breeze caressing your face. All of these provisions, plus so much more, are His ways of loving and showing you He cares about where you are and the details of your life. He is faithful right before your very eyes, you just have to look.

For You, LORD, bless the righteous one;
You surround him with favor like a shield.
Psalm 5:12

LORD, You have searched me and known me.
You know when I sit down and when I stand up. . . .
You have encircled me;
You have placed Your hand on me.
Psalm 139:1-2, 5

Happy are the people who are in such a state;
Happy are the people whose God is the LORD!
Psalm 144:15 NKJV

For Your faithful love is before my eyes,
and I live by Your truth.

Psalm 26:3

**PRAYER:**

Lord, Your faithfulness and love are immeasurable.
I know I can always count on You to provide what I need
each and every day. And I am so very grateful.

# REJOICE
# IN THE LORD

Rejoicing, praying, and expressing gratitude
is easy to do when life is going smoothly, but what
about when you're struggling just to get out of bed?
Jesus knew you'd have difficult times, and His antidote
for a stifled spirit is praise—not for the struggle, but for His presence
and promise of eternal life with Him. He loves you. He died for you.
And those are all the right reasons to rejoice in Him and be glad no
matter what.

He alone is your God,
the only One who is worthy of your praise,
the One who has done these mighty miracles
that you have seen with your own eyes.
Deuteronomy 10:21 NLT

Give thanks in everything,
for this is God's will for you in Christ Jesus.
I Thessalonians 5:18

Three times a day [Daniel] got down on his knees,
prayed, and gave thanks to his God,
just as he had done before.
Daniel 6:10

Rejoice always, pray without ceasing,
give thanks in all circumstances;
for this is the will of God
in Christ Jesus for you.
I Thessalonians 5:16-18 ESV

## PRAYER:

Jesus, I rejoice in You right now
and thank You from my heart for the sacrifice
You made on the cross for me. I am truly grateful.

# HE KNOWS, AND HE CARES

Do you ever have days or periods in life when no one seems to understand you? Perhaps you don't quite connect with others because they don't comprehend the kind of struggle you're going through. While reaching out to others for support is important, reaching up to the Savior is even more so. By God's grace, you are not only invited, you are called into fellowship with Jesus—His own Son. He knows exactly how you feel and is filled with compassion for you. His arms are open wide and waiting for your approach. Won't you run to Him now and receive His embrace?

May Your compassion come to me so that I may live,
for Your instruction is my delight.
Psalm 119:77 CSB

For we do not have a high priest
who is unable to sympathize with our weaknesses,
but One who has been tested
in every way as we are, yet without sin.
Hebrews 4:15

LORD, do not withhold Your compassion from me;
Your constant love and truth will always guard me.
Psalm 40:11

# day 18

God is faithful;
you were called by Him
into fellowship with His Son,
Jesus Christ our Lord.
I Corinthians 1:9

## PRAYER:

Jesus, thank You for being there for me.
Thank You for knowing exactly what I'm going through
and being willing to walk through it with me.
Thank You for reassuring me with Your care. You are a gift.

# IN THE RAW

Walk through any department store, watch TV, or peruse a magazine, and you're going to be faced with makeup ads. They tell, sell, and quell any securities about your looks, so you'll use their products to be more beautiful. And the ads work—the majority of women wear makeup to cover blemishes, enhance their best features, and . . . hide the stress and pain dwelling deep inside. But at the end of each day, after washing off the mask, there's just you in the mirror, in raw and real form. The makeup's job of appealing to the world is done. Now it's back to what God sees all along—a beautiful creation whom He loves and makes whole. No matter what you look like on the outside, God looks at your heart for Him, which is the most beautiful makeup you can ever wear.

For you formed my inward parts;
you knitted me together in my mother's womb.
I praise you, for I am fearfully and wonderfully made.
Wonderful are your works; my soul knows it very well.
Psalm 139:13-14 ESV

The precepts of the LORD are right,
making the heart glad; the command of the LORD is radiant,
making the eyes light up.
Psalm 19:8

The eye is the lamp of the body.
If your eye is good, your whole body will be full of light.
Matthew 6:22

The LORD said to Samuel, "Do not look at his appearance or at the height of his stature . . . for God sees not as man sees, for man looks at the outward appearance, but the LORD looks at the heart."

I Samuel 16:7 NASB

**PRAYER:**

Father, thank You that I don't have to look a certain way on the outside for You to love me. With the conditions set by this world, it's a hard concept to fully embrace. Please help me to really believe it and to flourish in the comfort of knowing I am loved just the way I am.

# PRAISE FOR SENSES

Smelling the scent of freshly baked bread . . .
hearing the coo of a newborn baby . . .
feeling the smoothness of a kitten's fur . . .
tasting the cold burst of your favorite ice cream . . .
seeing a gaze of love directed at you . . .

Have you ever wondered what life would be like without senses? It'd probably be like living in total darkness and with no stimuli. But with senses, life is exciting, because of all there is to see, touch, hear, smell, and taste. God gave us senses to enjoy Him and the display of His creation to the fullest from the time we are born to the time our eyes make a final close to sleep. What a thoughtful and caring God we have. Let us praise Him for His goodness through our senses.

Taste and see that the Lord is good.
How happy is the person who takes refuge in Him!
Psalm 34:8 CSB

You made all the delicate, inner parts of my body
and knit me together in my mother's womb. Thank
You for making me so wonderfully complex!
Psalm 139:13–14 NLT

You gave me a new song, a song of praise to You.
Many will see this, and they will honor
and trust You, the Lord God.
Psalm 40:3 CEV

He displayed His glory.

John 2:11

PRAYER:

Father, thank You for my senses and the sheer pleasure they bring. I am sorry I often take them for granted. I am so grateful for the ways You bless me through seeing, hearing, smelling, tasting, and feeling—especially for feeling the warmth of Your love all around.

# HE IS WATER OF LIFE

The steady flow of a waterfall cascading down and clapping onto a landing can be mesmerizing. There are big ones like Niagara Falls with such force, it's hard to comprehend the amount of power and speed within the rushing floods. Others are small trickles that pop out of stone walls only to vanish right back into the earth, leaving only a faint and soothing sound. Whether powerful or peaceful, they are beautiful reminders that God created an exquisite place for us to dwell. They represent life and cleansing, renewal and grace. The splendor they create are customized gifts to delight our hearts. They're only one of many parts of nature God gave us to enjoy and draw refreshment for our souls. Isn't He good?

He lets me lie down in green pastures;
He leads me beside quiet waters.
Psalm 23:2

The water I will give him will become a well
of water springing up within him for eternal life.
John 4:14

You will be like a watered garden
and like a spring whose waters never run dry.
Isaiah 58:11

He causes the springs to gush into the valleys;
they flow between the mountains.
They supply water for every wild beast.
Psalm 104:10-11

PRAYER:

Thank You, Lord, for the beauty of Your creation.
When I gaze on the work of Your hands,
my soul feels free from the burdens of
this world and at one with You.

# GOD HAS YOU COVERED

No doubt you woke up this morning with a problem that needs solving (because everyone has at least one problem). The good news is, whatever your need or solution, God has it covered. He knew you'd need help before you did. He's already been orchestrating circumstances in your life that will lead up to His provision. And not just for today's needs, but for every day's. He knows, and He provides in His perfect way, in His perfect time. The key now is to ask for His help. Don't be shy or bashful—He's ready for a full-on ask from a heart that trusts and believes He'll do what He says.

He has shown kindness by giving you rain
from heaven and crops in their seasons;
He provides you with plenty of food
and fills your hearts with joy.
Acts 14:17 NIV

For everyone who asks receives,
and the one who searches finds,
and to the one who knocks, the door will be opened.
What man among you, if his son asks him for bread,
will give him a stone?
Matthew 7:8–9

The LORD will always lead you,
satisfy you in a parched land.
Isaiah 58:11

Your Father knows what you need
before you ask Him.
Matthew 6:8 NIV

## PRAYER:

Father God, thank You for knowing me so well
that You know what I need before I do.
I ask for Your help now and trust You
to work out the many details of
what I'm facing on my behalf.

# ANOTHER KIND OF GRACE

Grace . . . It's a gift from God for every believer the instant they receive Christ as Savior. But there's another kind of grace that isn't received—it is said. It's the offering of thanksgiving before a meal. This form of grace comes from the Latin *gratiarum actio*, which means "act of thanks." Jesus said grace—from the feeding of the five thousand to the Last Supper—to set the example for us to follow. But in our hurried pace, it's easy to skip saying and go right to consuming without a second thought. To honor our Lord, saying grace is a simple, sweet, and divine outward expression of the glad and heartfelt gratefulness within. So let us remember not only to live in grace, but to say it too.

Then [Jesus] took the five loaves and the two fish,
and looking up to heaven,
He blessed and broke the loaves.
Mark 6:41

As they were eating, Jesus took bread,
blessed and broke it, [and] gave it to the disciples. . .
Then He took a cup, and after giving thanks,
He gave it to them.
Matthew 26:26-27

Then [Jesus] took the seven loaves,
thanked God for them, broke them into pieces
and passed them to His disciples.
Mark 8:6 TLB

And day by day, attending the temple together
and breaking bread in their homes,
[the apostles] received their food
with glad and generous hearts.

**Acts 2:46 ESV**

**PRAYER:**

Father, because of Your provision, I eat and am nourished.
I know there are many who starve, yet You fill my plate.
Thank You for Your abundance—may I never take it for granted.

# THE WALKING DEAD

*The Walking Dead* . . . It's a dark, popular TV show, but let's think about the concept of these words in a spiritual light. Going through life on your own, having no real purpose, achieving goals that don't bring lasting fulfillment, facing eternal consequences of sin . . . that kind of living is void of life. It is living in death, or, walking dead. But knowing Christ brings life to the soul—He is life. He gives new purpose, new meaning, a new mind, a new slate. Christ didn't come to turn bad people into good, He came to give life to the dead. By God's grace, He literally transforms dried-up, withered beings into mighty oaks of righteousness for eternity. That is something to be thankful for.

The Spirit of the Sovereign Lord is on me,
because the Lord has anointed me . . .
to bestow . . . the oil of joy instead of mourning,
and a garment of praise instead of a spirit of despair.
They will be called oaks of righteousness,
a planting of the Lord for the display of His splendor.
Isaiah 61:1, 3-4 NIV

We were buried therefore with Him by baptism into death,
in order that, just as Christ was raised
from the dead by the glory of the Father,
we too might walk in newness of life.
Romans 6:4 ESV

But God, who is rich in mercy,
because of His great love that He had for us,
made us alive with the Messiah
even though we were dead in trespasses.
You are saved by grace!

Ephesians 2:5 NIV

## PRAYER:

Lord Jesus, thank You for the life and purpose
You've given to me. I pray You will make my life
a display of Your splendor for all the world to see.

# MERCY TRIUMPHS

Mercy triumphs, thanks be to God. That means, instead of God judging and condemning you for any wrongdoing, He extends His mercy. Think of a time you did something you knew you shouldn't have. Then the agonizing moments of waiting to receive your punishment. Perhaps you're there now . . . Oh, but God isn't a punisher. When you have a repentant heart—when you agree with Him that you were wrong—He lavishes His mercy around you like a warm blanket to catch your fall and to heal your heart. No condemnation—Jesus took that on Himself, so you wouldn't have to. Praise God for His mercy.

The one who conceals his sins
will not prosper,
but whoever confesses and renounces them
will find mercy.
Proverbs 28:13

I [Jesus] desire mercy and not sacrifice.
For I didn't come to call the righteous, but sinners.
Matthew 9:13

His mercy goes on from generation to generation,
to all who reverence Him.
Luke 1:50 TLB

Mercy triumphs over judgment.
James 2:13

Father, I am so sorry for the ways I fall down and disappoint You.
I am so grateful for Your understanding and mercy that covers
me with the security and comfort of Your never-ending love.

# LET'S CELEBRATE!

God likes a good celebration as much as we do—and we have all kinds of reasons and excuses to do just that. There are typical birthdays, holidays, and graduations. But there are also other occasions, such as being two years cancer free, or one year free from the bondage of alcohol or drugs. There are holy celebrations throughout the Old Testament and current-day occurrences, such as the day each of us accepted Christ as our personal Savior. That's something to celebrate no matter what day it is. Let us praise from the heavens and let God know how much He is loved for what He has done. Giving thanks for sacrificing His Son for all of humankind is the very least we can do. Shout hallelujah!

The righteous are glad; they rejoice before God and
celebrate with joy. Sing to God! Sing praises to His name.
Exalt Him who rides on the clouds—
His name is Yahweh—and rejoice before Him.
Psalm 68:3–4

"This day is to be a memorial for you,
and you must celebrate it as a festival to the Lord.
You are to celebrate it throughout
your generations as a permanent statute."
Exodus 12:14

"Let's celebrate with a feast,
because this son of mine was dead and is alive again;
he was lost and is found!" So they began to celebrate.
Luke 15:23–24

Hallelujah!
Praise the LORD from the heavens;
praise Him in the heights.
Psalm 148:1

## PRAYER:

Father, thank You from the top of my lungs and the bottom of my heart for saving me, for covering my sins with Your grace, and for the eternal hope of heaven I have with You.

# PRAISE OVER PLEADING

There will always be a problem in life to pray about, so why can't there always be something in life to praise about? Another way to look at it is, if praise time got equal time with the pleading and petitioning, the hard times wouldn't seem so hard. There certainly isn't anything to lose by giving thanks, and there's everything to gain by doing it—such as a lighter heart filled with more peace and contentment.

You are not in control—praise God that He is. You don't know next steps to take—praise God that He does. You wonder if God's love will ever end—give thanks that His love endures forever.

Give thanks to the LORD,
for He is good and His loyal love endures.
I Chronicles 16:34 NET

My tongue will proclaim Your righteousness,
Your praise all day long.
Psalm 35:28

Praise Him in His mighty heavens.
Praise Him for His powerful acts;
praise Him for His abundant greatness. . . .
Let everything that breathes praise the LORD.
Hallelujah!
Psalm 150:1-2, 6

Give thanks to the Lord,
for He is good;
His love endures forever.
Psalm 106:1 NIV

PRAYER:

Father, I love You, I worship You,
I praise You from the depths of my being.
You alone are worthy to be praised
each and every day of life.

# SINGING IN THE RAIN

Robins are fun and inspiring birds. They're fun because they are sufficiently bold to land close enough for you to observe their movements and quirky expressions. They tilt their heads to scope for worms and bounce around as though they are king of the land. They're inspiring because, in the spring and summer months, whenever it rains, they will sing—in the rain. Hearing their song in the rain is a good reminder to give thanks and praise to God even when it is raining in life. Not only will your own heart be glad, others will take notice and maybe even start singing too. If robins are mindful enough to sing to their Creator while clouds hover and water falls, we can be as well.

The birds of the sky live beside the springs;
they sing among the foliage.
Psalm 104:12

I will sing of Your strength and will joyfully proclaim
Your faithful love in the morning.
For You have been a stronghold for me,
a refuge in my day of trouble.
Psalm 59:16 CSB

Sing a new song to the Lord; sing to the Lord, all the earth.
Sing to Yahweh, praise His name;
proclaim His salvation from day to day.
Declare His glory among the nations,
His wonderful works among all peoples.
Psalm 96:1-3

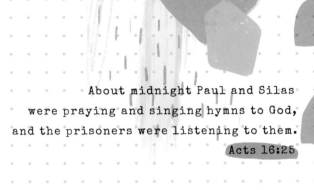

About midnight Paul and Silas
were praying and singing hymns to God,
and the prisoners were listening to them.

Acts 16:25

Father, thank You for birdsong to brighten my day.
I will sing my praise to You now,
even in the rain of all my troubles.

Hallelujah, amen.

# NEW MERCIES
# EVERY MORNING

Imagine lying in bed at night, wrapped up in your sheets, and replaying the day in your mind—all the things you wished you'd done or said differently. Or maybe your soul is downcast because of an overwhelming problem. You may even wish you could hit replay and start all over. Well, you can. With each new dawn, God's love and mercies are there waiting for you to soak them in and start anew. Yesterday and its regrets are over, and His faithfulness and love are still burning strong with each new morning.

I have trusted in Your faithful love;
my heart will rejoice in Your deliverance.
Psalm 13:5

Praise be to the God and Father of our Lord Jesus Christ.
God is the Father Who is full of mercy and all comfort.
II Corinthians 1:3 NCV

Give thanks to the LORD, for He is good;
His faithful love endures forever.
I Chronicles 16:34

The steadfast love
of the Lord never ceases;
his mercies never come to an end;
they are new every morning;
great is your faithfulness.
Lamentations 3:22-23 ESV

**PRAYER:**

Father, I am thankful and relieved that,
because You love me so much, Your new mercies
abound in my life every day.

# GOD'S BIGGER PURPOSE

Butterflies and bees . . . they are both workers in more ways than one. While they are busy floating from flower to flower drinking in nectar, they are also cross pollinating. Their focus is on the nectar, but they're actually performing a miracle by creation without even knowing it. That is the way God works in your life too. While you are zeroed in on a specific task, such as simply going to work, He is working a bigger picture of touching others and blessing them in ways that you don't realize. It could be through a casual conversation in an elevator, or an email that conveys patience instead of pressure. God is constantly working in ways you don't see, which is good reason to let your light shine, even in the small things, and rejoice in being a servant of the King.

Whatever you do, do it from the heart,
as something done for the Lord and not for people.
Colossians 3:23 CSB

Let your light shine in front of men.
Then they will see the good things you do and
will honor your Father Who is in heaven.
Matthew 5:16 NLV

Throw yourselves into the work of the Master,
confident that nothing you do for Him
is a waste of time or effort.
I Corinthians 15:58 THE MESSAGE

Serve the LORD with gladness . . . .
Psalm 100:2

day

30

PRAYER:

Father, You are divine and too great for me to understand.
But I trust You and hope to act and speak in ways that
are pleasing and bring You glory to those around me.

# HE IS JEALOUS FOR YOU

Have you ever been jealous? If you have, then you know the hurt when someone you want attention from gives it to someone else. You can be a parent who misses a child that would rather spend time with friends, or your best friend moved away and doesn't keep in touch because she's made new friends. The bottom line is, they would rather be somewhere else or with someone else, and it hurts. Have you thought that Jesus feels much the same? He loves you and yearns for time and attention with you. You're not just any other grain of sand on a beach. You are special to Him. He wants you to be with Him to share about your life and receive His love today, tomorrow, and the next. He is jealous for you.

You are never to bow down to another god
because Yahweh, being jealous by nature,
is a jealous God.
Exodus 34:14

You were called by Him into fellowship . . . .
I Corinthians 1:9

But as for me,
God's presence is my good.
Psalm 73:28

Do you think it's without reason
the Scripture says that the Spirit
who lives in us yearns jealously?

James 4:5

**PRAYER:**

Lord, thank You for loving me so much that You literally yearn
to be with me. I want to be with You now because You are the
One true, stable source of peace and fulfillment in my life.

# LOVE NOTES

Imagine all the singing and worship to God that takes place every day on our planet. Start at Greenwich, England, where each new day begins, and, as the earth rotates, new waves of worship burst forth with each time zone. That means there is singing and praise to God being heard from around the world throughout the entire day. Oh, the pleasure this must bring His Majesty, especially on Sundays! The next time you start singing, whether in the shower, in your car, or in church, you are joining the great choir of the masses and blessing the heart of the One who is in the heavens. Be assured, He hears and loves every note.

O sing to the Lord a new song;
Sing to the Lord, all the earth!
Psalm 96:1 AMP

I will sing; I will sing praises
with the whole of my being.
Psalm 108:1

To You, my God, I will sing a new song;
I will sing Your sweet praises.
Psalm 144:9 VOICE

Sing to the LORD, all the earth.
Proclaim His salvation from day to day.
I Chronicles 16:23

**PRAYER:**

Father in heaven, I lift my voice to You today to praise
and worship You as my Creator, my Redeemer, my Savior,
and my Friend. My heart is full of song for You.

# THE WONDER OF STARS

It's been said that there are more stars in the universe than there are grains of sand on all the beaches of the world. That seems unfathomable, yet with modern-day telescopes, we are learning that this is true. What's special is, the stars we see today are the same stars Moses, King David, the disciples, and other great heroes of the past gazed upon. God has passed the stars' torch of burning brightness from the beginning of time for us to enjoy and carry in our hearts today. Let us praise Him along with the stars by shining with the brightness of His glory and His love.

He alone stretches out the heavens
and treads on the waves of the sea.
He makes the stars: the Bear, Orion,
the Pleiades, and the constellations of the southern sky.
He does great and unsearchable things,
wonders without number.
Job 9:8–10

He merely spoke,
and the heavens were formed and
all the galaxies of stars.
Psalm 33:6 TLB

There is a splendor of the sun, another of the moon,
and another of the stars; for one star differs
from another star in splendor.
I Corinthians 15:41

day

## 33

Praise Him, sun and moon;
praise Him, all you shining stars.
Psalm 148:3

### PRAYER:

Father, thank You for the stars in the heavens on which
we can gaze and be amazed. They are a shining testament
to Your creativity, and happy reminders of Your love and
Your presence from the beginning of time into eternity.

# GET A GOOD GRIP

What do golfing, fishing, and swinging a hammer have in common? They all require a grip to accomplish your goal. And not just any grip, but a tight one so that when you swing the pole or club, it remains solid in your hand for the very best contact. Success in your life and faith are the same. In order to do and be your very best and not get thrown off balance or knocked down, you've got to keep a firm and steadfast hold on the promises God has for you. His Word is truth and provides a solid foundation for all that you do. So hold strong, cling to His truths, and get ready for making an impact for God's Kingdom like never before.

Sing a new song to Him;
play skillfully on the strings, with a joyful shout.
For the word of the LORD is right,
and all His work is trustworthy.
Psalm 33:3-4

Then the people believed what the LORD said,
and they sang praises to Him.
Psalm 106:12 NCV

I wait for the LORD;
I wait and put my hope in His word.
Psalm 130:5 CSB

"Your heart must hold on to My words.
Keep My commands and live."

Proverbs 4:4

Lord, thank You for the promises in Your Word for me
to hold on to. I will cling to them and claim them as
my very own this day, tomorrow, and the next.

# REACH FOR GOD

There's nothing quite so heartwarming as a newborn baby to cuddle in your arms. The coos, the sweet smell, the soft-gazing eyes looking into yours . . . When you touch her little fingers, they'll wrap around yours in complete acceptance and trust as if to say, "Hi. I love you too." And just as you reach for a baby's hand, God extends Himself to you each day for you to accept and wrap your heart around His. He wants to keep you in the safety of His presence. He loves you, He created you, and He wants you to have complete and restful trust and love for Him. You are sheltered and secure in His arms. Won't you reach for Him today?

He reached down from above and took hold of me . . . .
Psalm 18:16 NET

Jesus, however, invited them:
"Let the little children come to Me,
and don't stop them, because the kingdom
of God belongs to such as these."
Luke 18:16

I call to God Most High, to God who fulfills
His purpose for me. He reaches down
from heaven and saves me.
Psalm 57:2-3 CSB

day

35

We are a sweet smell of Christ
that reaches up to God.
II Corinthians 2:15 NLV

PRAYER:

Father, I reach to You right now and rest
in Your presence. I release all of my concerns
to Your mighty hand and walk in the peace
that knowing You gives.

# CAST YOUR BURDENS

What weighs on your mind today? What is pulling your spirit in different directions and wearing you out? Dear one, God knows about them all. And He understands that you are weak and can only handle so much at one time. That's why He promises to help—He will carry your burdens for you. There's no time or weight limit to make Him say, "You've reached your quota for the day." His strength is limitless, and no amount of trouble is too hard for Him. He finds great pleasure in helping and caring for your every need. But you've first got to cast them into His hands, then trust and rest in knowing He's got them under control.

Give your burdens to the LORD,
and He will take care of you.
Psalm 55:22 NLT

Then Jesus said, "Come to Me, all of you who are weary
and carry heavy burdens, and I will give you rest."
Matthew 11:28 NLT

Be courageous! I have conquered the world.
John 16:33

I will rejoice and be glad in Your faithful love
because You have seen my affliction.
You have known the troubles of my life.
Psalm 31:7

Thanks be to the LORD,
who daily carries our burdens for us.
God is our salvation.
Psalm 68:19 GW

Lord, thank You for Your grace and strength to carry me
through this day. I give You my burdens now and rest in
knowing You have taken them, and that You are with me.

# CHRIST'S RESURRECTION AND YOU

You've probably read or been told that you are not defined by your past mistakes. And it's true, you aren't. Your failures or heartaches may shape who you are, but they do not define you. The question now is, what are you defined by? The most important thing that separates you as a Christian from other faiths is the resurrection of Jesus. It is the pivotal factor that has created arguments and dissension among people for centuries. Jesus's defining moment of the resurrection is what defines you too. He rose from the dead, and you did too when you accepted Him into your heart. So live forward in freedom.

Having been buried with Him in baptism,
you were also raised with Him through faith
in the working of God, who raised Him from the dead.
Colossians 2:12

Praise the God and Father of our Lord Jesus Christ.
According to His great mercy, He has given us a new birth
into a living hope through the resurrection
of Jesus Christ from the dead.
I Peter 1:3

And the dead man came out, his hands and feet bound
in graveclothes, his face wrapped in a headcloth.
Jesus told them, "Unwrap him and let him go!"
John 11:44 NLT

For if we have been joined with Him
in the likeness of His death,
we will certainly also be in
the likeness of His resurrection.

Romans 6:5

## PRAYER:

Father, thank You for the resurrection and the life that
is in me because of Jesus. I love You for blessing me with
such a great gift—the promise of new life today and
spending eternity with You in all my tomorrows.

# GOD'S PURPOSE FOR YOU

Inhaling a deep breath after a fresh spring rain, listening to morning birds bursting forth in praise, being still and relishing quiet time with God—all of these experiences bring moments of delight in the Lord. And as you spend more and more time in His creation, in His Word, in prayer, He plants seeds of desire for His purposes for you. As you give Him your heart, He sings back to yours, calling you to fulfill the exact purpose He's created you for. It will be more than you could ever imagine—you are a masterpiece in the making.

For it is God who is working in you,
enabling you both to desire and to work out
His good purpose.
Philippians 2:13

"For I know the plans I have for you,"
declares the Lord, "plans to prosper you and
not to harm you, plans to give you
hope and a future."
Jeremiah 29:11 NIV

He who started a good work in you
will carry it on to completion
until the day of Christ Jesus.
Philippians 1:6

Delight yourself in the LORD,
and he will give you
the desires of your heart.
Psalm 37:4 ESV

O Father, I love being in Your presence
and soaking in the peace and love You have for me.
I want what You want for me because I know it's the very best.

# NO GREATER LOVE

When someone says they love you, you can tell over time whether or not they are sincere by observing their actions. If his or her gestures don't reflect love, the words are empty and have no significance. But when they go out of their way time after time, you can rest assured they are serious. That's why it's easy to trust and believe God when He says He loves you—His actions day after day prove His love to be the greatest and most genuine. He not only sent His Son, Jesus, to be your personal Savior, He sacrificed Him on a cross for you. He gave his life . . . for you. There is no greater form of love than to give one's life on behalf of another. Praise Him today, give thanks for what He has done, and be glad.

I am the good shepherd.
The good shepherd lays down his life for the sheep.
John 10:11 NIV

Grace was given to us through Christ Jesus before time began,
but it is now shown to us by the coming of
our Savior Christ Jesus. He destroyed death,
and through the Good News He showed us the way
to have life that cannot be destroyed.
II Timothy 1:9-10 NCV

I have trusted in Your faithful love;
my heart will rejoice in Your deliverance.
I will sing to the Lord because He has treated me generously.
Psalm 13:5-6

# day 39

For God loved the world in this way:
He gave His One and Only Son,
so that everyone who believes in Him
will not perish but have eternal life.
John 3:16

## PRAYER:

Father, words cannot express my gratitude
for my very salvation. Thanks be to Jesus's sacrifice,
so I can spend eternity with You.
There is no greater love I've ever known.

# YOU ARE PRICELESS

When cleaning out a closet or an attic, a lot of time can be spent thinking about whether an item is worth keeping or if it's time to throw it away. The more value or sentiment the piece has, the better the chance you'll keep it. Otherwise, it goes to the nearest thrift store or the trash. Isn't it wonderful that, when God looks at you, He doesn't compare your worth with someone else's. That's because you are already of the highest quality. By His grace, you are as priceless now as the day you came into existence. No one compares to you because you are a child of the King—you were fearfully and wonderfully made. Your value is exquisite and that of royalty. To God, you are a keeper . . . from now to eternity.

But you are A CHOSEN RACE, A royal PRIESTHOOD,
A CONSECRATED NATION, A [special] PEOPLE FOR *God's* OWN POSSESSION, so
that you may proclaim the excellencies
[the wonderful deeds and virtues and perfections]
of Him who called you out of darkness into His marvelous light.
I Peter 2:9 AMP

The LORD their God will save them on that day
as the flock of His people; for they are like jewels
in a crown, sparkling over His land.
Zechariah 9:16

The Spirit Himself testifies together with our spirit
that we are God's children, and if children, also
heirs—heirs of God and coheirs with Christ.
Romans 8:16-17

## day 40

I praise you, for I am fearfully
and wonderfully made.
Wonderful are your works;
my soul knows it very well.

Psalm 139:14 ESV

**PRAYER:**

Lord, my worth isn't as important to anyone
as much as it is to You. After all, You created me!
Thank You for the gift of knowing I am cherished and loved.

# WHAT'S YOUR FOCUS?

If you've ever walked through a model home, you can tell it's been professionally staged—the furniture and décor are perfectly arranged in relation to each room's focal point. There's no confusing the purpose for each space, and the flow from room to room is natural and smooth. Similarly, when you begin each day focusing your thoughts on God's goodness and aligning your day according to His will, your purpose becomes fixed on the solid foundation of His love. You are then able to flow from moment to moment, task to task, with a supernatural ease and peace throughout your day—regardless of what happens. Keep your eyes on Jesus.

If you accept My words and store up My commands within you, listening closely to wisdom and directing your heart to understanding . . . then you will understand the fear of the Lord and discover the knowledge of God. For the Lord gives wisdom; from His mouth come knowledge and understanding. Proverbs 2:1-6

Because of our God's tender mercy the dawn will break upon us from on high to give light to those who sit in darkness and in the shadow of death, to guide our feet into the way of peace.
Luke 1:78-79 NET

# day 41

Let us run the race that is before us
and never give up . . . .
Let us look only to Jesus,
the One who began our faith
and who makes it perfect.
Hebrews 12:1-2 NCV

PRAYER:

Lord, I just want to see You. Please block out
all things that are not of You, and help me focus
on Your will, Your way, and Your truth for this day.

# THE SHAPE OF YOUR HEART

What is the shape of your heart? Seriously, if you were to describe your heart, what would it look like? About to pop, or deflated? Strong and vital, or crushed and weak? Would there be a hole, or have cracks? No matter what shape or condition you think it's in, as a child of the King, you have access to the fullness of God's grace to flow into every heartbeat to smooth every rough edge, and to heal every cut and bruise. When you live with a heart shaped by God and for God, His gifts of healing, hope, and life transform the shape of any heart into one of absolute beauty.

The Spirit of the Lord God is on me,
because the Lord has anointed me
to bring good news to the poor.
He has sent Me to heal the brokenhearted . . .
to comfort all who mourn . . .
to give them a crown of beauty instead of ashes,
festive oil instead of mourning,
and splendid clothes instead of despair.
Isaiah 61:1–3

He heals the brokenhearted
and binds up their wounds.
Psalm 147:3

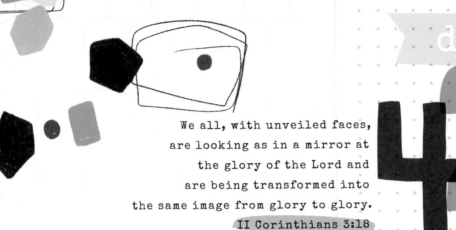

42

We all, with unveiled faces,
are looking as in a mirror at
the glory of the Lord and
are being transformed into
the same image from glory to glory.
II Corinthians 3:18

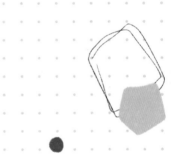

PRAYER:

Father, You are Healer of all wounds,
Life-giver to the lost, and Savior of all of humanity.
Thank You for Your healing grace and a hope-filled heart.

# ALONE WITH GOD

If you're an introvert, you know full well that being around people quickly saps your energy—and the antidote for regeneration is to retreat alone to the quiet. If you're an extrovert, the opposite is the case: you're energized by being around others—socializing is what gives you energy and satisfaction. But whichever you are, the only way to truly fill your cup of completeness is by spending time alone with God. Being still in His presence is the only source that genuinely fills your heart and mind with the rest, strength, power, and wisdom needed for a successful and balanced life.

God, Your faithful love is so valuable
that people take refuge in the shadow of Your wings.
They are filled from the abundance of Your house;
You let them drink from Your refreshing stream,
for with You is life's fountain.
Psalm 36:7-9

He said to them,
"Come away by yourselves to a remote place
and rest for a while."
Mark 6:31

The God of all grace, the One who called you
into His eternal glory in Christ Jesus,
will Himself restore, empower,
strengthen, and establish you.
I Peter 5:10 CEB

day

43

He says, "Stop your striving and
recognize that I am God!"
Psalm 46:10 NET

PRAYER:

Father, I come to You now and stop.
I ascribe to You the glory due Your name,
and rest in Your glorious presence.
I come to You and rest.

# PUT ON JESUS

Isn't it a marvel that God provides not just any armor for your daily spiritual survival, He provides the *full* armor of Jesus. It covers every inch—there are no spaces for even the smallest darts from the enemy to slip through. Each piece is divinely anointed to cover you with His strength as soon as you put it on. God knows and understands the battles that rage within and around you, whether they be inward—discouragement or fear—or outward—a questionable place or person. He will shield out whatever prevents you from experiencing complete peace. Rejoice that you can walk in full confidence today, and every day, under the protection of His power and grace.

David said to the Philistine:
"You come against me with a dagger, spear, and sword,
but I come against you in the name of Yahweh of Hosts."
I Samuel 17:45

My shield is with God,
who saves the upright in heart.
Psalm 7:10

For our battle is not against flesh and blood,
but against the rulers, against the authorities,
against the world powers of this darkness,
against the spiritual forces of evil in the heavens.
Ephesians 6:12

Be strengthened by the Lord
and by His vast strength.
Put on the full armor of God
so that you can stand against
the tactics of the Devil.
Ephesians 6:10-11

**PRAYER:**

Lord, thank You for the gift of Your mighty armor.
I love knowing that I can walk and live every day
within the safety of Your full protection,
in ways that repel the enemy and lead me to victory.

# COMPASSIONATE GOD

We've all done it . . . that is, done something foolish or harmful without realizing just how wrong we were for doing it—until it was too late. Those are the times you want everyone to go away so you can crawl into a hole and hide your face. They are also times when your heavenly Father loves to reach down and wrap you in His arms and say, "It's okay. I love you anyway." He shows up to cover your mistakes with a soothing balm of grace to heal your broken spirit. He is a God of compassion, not ridicule; a God to run to, not run from.

> Do not withhold Your compassion
> and tender mercy from me, O LORD;
> Your lovingkindness and Your truth
> will continually preserve me.
> Psalm 40:11 AMP

> My heart says this about You, "You are to seek My face."
> LORD, I will seek Your face. Do not hide Your face from me;
> do not turn Your servant away in anger. You have been my helper;
> do not leave me or abandon me, God of my salvation.
> Even if my father and mother abandon me,
> the LORD cares for me.
> Psalm 27:8-10

> You, LORD, are a compassionate and gracious God,
> slow to anger and rich in faithful love and truth.
> Turn to me and be gracious to me.
> Psalm 86:15-16

I received mercy because
I acted out of ignorance in unbelief.
And the grace of our Lord overflowed,
along with the faith and love
that are in Christ Jesus.
I Timothy 1:13-14

PRAYER:

Father, thank You for covering me with Your mercy
and grace after I've blown it. Help me to know better
next time and extend the same blessing to others.

# HOPE IS . . .

Hope is . . . believing for what you do not yet see. Sometimes it's easy to have hope because everything is moving straight toward the finish line of your dream—that's happy hope. Other times, circumstances look so bleak, there is little hope left—or waning hope. But, when you trust in the God of hope and not in the results of what is hoped for, you can have hope overflowing with peace and joy because the outcome is in His perfect hands—that's holy hope. He is the one, true Source of perfect hope and perfect peace.

LORD, when doubts fill my mind,
when my heart is in turmoil,
quiet me and give me renewed hope and cheer.
Psalm 94:19 TLB

So don't lose hope.
I, the LORD, have spoken.
Jeremiah 31:17 CEV

But since we belong to the day,
we must be serious and put the armor of faith
and love on our chests,
and put on a helmet of the hope of salvation.
I Thessalonians 5:8

Now may the God of hope fill you with all joy
and peace as you believe in Him
so that you may overflow with hope
by the power of the Holy Spirit.
Romans 15:13

PRAYER:

Dear Lord, You are the one, true Source
of genuine hope everlasting. Please fill me with
all hope for a victorious day, week, year, and
life. My hope is in You and You alone.

# HIS WORD IS FOR YOU

When you go to your mailbox and pull out the mail, the first thing you naturally do is look at the return address. If it's from the power company, it's a bill to collect money. If it's from a friend, it's probably a sweet card. If it's from a stranger, you quickly determine if it's junk or worthy of opening. In all cases, you are filtering the intent of the sender. But when it comes to opening the Bible, you can rest in knowing that the Author had your very best interest at heart. He wants you to know Him and His promises; to know of the salvation He offers, and that His love and grace are abundantly yours. His Word is truth, it is eternal, and it was written just for you. Will you read it?

God—His way is perfect;
the word of the LORD is pure.
He is a shield to all who take refuge in Him.
For who is God besides Yahweh?
And who is a rock? Only our God.
Psalm 18:30-31

Lord GOD, You are God; Your words are true,
and You have promised this grace to Your servant.
II Samuel 7:28

Heaven and earth will pass away,
but My words will never pass away.
Mark 13:31

Now the Word became flesh and
took up residence among us. We saw His glory—
the glory of the one and only,
full of grace and truth,
who came from the Father.
John 1:14 NET

Father, thank You for the gift of Your Word,
and that I can trust every part of it for my good.
I will read it, cherish it, and commit to applying
Your love and wisdom to my life.

# LIVE IN THE FULLNESS OF TODAY

One of the hardest things to do is not worry about tomorrow. There are so many "what-ifs" that could happen. What if I don't get well? What if there's not enough money for the month? What if I fail? The list can be endless. Instead of fretting about the what-ifs, consider giving thanks about tomorrow and the ways God will reveal His faithfulness. You don't know what tomorrow brings, but He does. And if you really believe that God is good and that He is working for your good, then you can rest in knowing He will provide, protect, and act in the ways you need. So praise God for what He has already done for tomorrow, then turn your focus on today and live life to the fullest right now.

Therefore I tell you, don't worry about your life,
what you will eat; or about the body, what you will wear.
Luke 12:22

Seek first the kingdom of God and His righteousness,
and all these things will be provided for you.
Therefore don't worry about tomorrow,
because tomorrow will worry about itself.
Matthew 6:33-34

Don't worry about your life.
Matthew 6:25

Don't worry about anything, but in everything,
through prayer and petition with thanksgiving,
let your requests be made known to God.

Philippians 4:6

## PRAYER:

Dear Lord, help me to worry less and trust You more.
You have blessed my life until now,
and I believe You will uphold me to face tomorrow.

# THE LIGHT OF LIFE

Did you know that light was the starting point of creation? That is because God is light, and God is the Creator of the universe. What's amazing is, light has energy like no other. It travels at 186 thousand miles per second—that's 670 million miles per hour! That example alone shows the greatness of God's energy and power in a meager way for human minds to comprehend. God beams with His power and strength around us every day at incredible speed and force. His light reveals His beauty, His supremacy, and His all-encompassing love through Jesus. Bask in His light, soak in His splendor, take in the radiance of His love for you today.

Then God said, "Let there be light,"
and there was light.
Genesis 1:3

The Son is the radiance of God's glory
and the exact expression of His nature,
sustaining all things by His powerful word.
Hebrews 1:3

I am the light of the world.
Anyone who follows Me will never walk in the darkness
but will have the light of life.
John 8:12

**day**

**49**

God is light,
and there is absolutely
no darkness in Him.
I John 1:5

**PRAYER:**

Father, thank You for the light of Your love
that shines all around me. Help me to soak it in
and radiate beams of Your light and love onto others.

# SAVIOR OF THE WORLD

Jesus . . .

He rescues us from trouble;

He redeems time lost to sin;

He breaks the chains that bind;

He delivers from distress;

He sends His Word to guide;

He stills the storms of life;

He sets the enslaved free;

He guides us to safe pasture;

He blesses the work of our hands;

He heals the brokenhearted;

He lifts the needy out of suffering;

He leads us on right paths;

He satisfies parched souls;

He offers grace to the punishable;

He shines His light on darkness;

He comforts when we mourn;

He forgives when we repent;

He loves when we're unlovable;

He saves a lost humanity;

He died so we can live.

He is the Savior of the world.

I, I am Yahweh, and there is no other Savior but Me.
Isaiah 43:11

God exalted this man to His right hand as ruler and Savior,
to grant repentance to Israel, and forgiveness of sins.
Acts 5:31

day
50

Give thanks to the LORD, for He is good;
His faithful love endures forever.
Psalm 107:1

PRAYER:

I thank You and praise You, Jesus,
for Your greatness, Your goodness,
Your faithfulness, and Your love.
No one and nothing compares.

# GOD'S SPIRIT IN YOU

If you have asked Jesus to be your Savior, it means He is in you. You are literally filled with His Spirit—yes, God's Spirit, the Creator of the universe. His Spirit is not just a thin drip line to call on when needed, it's a full-on maximum occupancy to draw from 24/7. He resides in your heart, your spirit, your very being to fill every void, heal every wound, and calm every nerve that has been damaged and left for dead. You are alive in Him to be strengthened and renewed, restored and refreshed for the rest of your life. When Jesus died, He left a part of Himself for you. Praise His holy name.

Don't you yourselves know that you are God's sanctuary
and that the Spirit of God lives in you?
I Corinthians 3:16

For the entire fullness of God's nature
dwells bodily in Christ,
and you have been filled by Him.
Colossians 2:9–10

We are here to tell you about all this,
and so is the Holy Spirit,
who is God's gift to everyone who obeys God.
Acts 5:32 CEV

This hope will not disappoint us,
because God's love has been poured out in our hearts
through the Holy Spirit who was given to us.
Romans 5:5

5

The Spirit of God, who raised
Jesus from the dead, lives in you.
Romans 8:11 NLT

PRAYER:

Father, to know that Your Spirit dwells within me is almost
unfathomable. I know I don't draw boldness and courage from You
to the level that I could. But I want to begin today embracing
the power You provide like no other. Thank You for this gift!

# GOD'S PROMISES
# ARE TRUE

There aren't many people in life who will keep their word 100 percent of the time. But when God says something, it's true. Has He said He has a purpose for your life? He does. Has He promised to provide for your every need? He will. Has He said He'd be with you wherever you go? He's there. Did He say that nothing will separate you from His love? Then nothing will. Is His grace sufficient for you? It is.

If He said it, it's true.

All the paths of the Lord are loving and true
for those who keep His agreement and keep His Laws.
Psalm 25:10 NLV

You will know the truth,
and the truth will set you free.
John 8:32

They sent their disciples to him,
along with the Herodians, saying,
"Teacher, we know that you are true and teach the way
of God truthfully, and you do not care
about anyone's opinion."
Matthew 22:16 ESV

The One who called you
is completely dependable.
If He said it, He'll do it!
I Thessalonians 5:24 THE MESSAGE

**PRAYER:**

Lord, I am so grateful that I can trust You completely and
know with full confidence that Your Word is Your bond. The
more I depend on You, the more I rest in Your truth.

# GRACE FOR A LIFETIME

Thank goodness for grace periods. If you're a few days late paying a bill, there's a five-day grace period, so there won't be a penalty. If you purchase an item, take it home, then decide you don't want it, there's a thirty-day grace period to return it and get your money back. But the best grace period of all is the one we have under the covering of God's love and through His Son, Jesus. It lasts a lifetime. God's grace period is stamped: ETERNITY.

Indeed, we have all received grace after grace
from His fullness,
for the law was given through Moses,
grace and truth came through Jesus Christ.
John 1:16–17

And now I entrust you to God and
the message of His grace that is able to build you up
and give you an inheritance with all those
He has set apart for Himself.
Acts 20:32 NLT

Since by the one man's trespass,
death reigned through that one man,
how much more will those who receive the overflow
of grace and the gift of righteousness reign
in life through the one man, Jesus Christ.
Romans 5:17

We have redemption in Him through His blood,
the forgiveness of our trespasses,
according to the riches of His grace
that He lavished on us with all
wisdom and understanding.
Ephesians 1:7-8

## PRAYER:

Thank You, Father, for covering me,
my life, my sin, my everything with Your grace,
so that I may spend eternity with You.

# ARM YOURSELF

Watching TV can be tricky. Innocent-looking shows can suddenly turn inappropriate, and commercials bombard you with higher volume and tacky sales pitches. Thank goodness for the fast forward and mute buttons! As long as the remote control is nearby, you can eliminate the distractions and enticements with the touch of a finger. This is the case with quoting Scripture. When suddenly faced with temptation or ungodly thoughts, quoting a verse from God's Word has the power to eliminate its pull within seconds. So, be prepared. Arm yourself in advance with key Scripture. By God's grace, hold on to the authority you have in His Word, and use it.

The tempter approached [Jesus] and said,
"If You are the Son of God, tell these stones to become bread."
But He answered, "It is written: Man must not
live on bread alone but on every word that comes
from the mouth of God" [Deuteronomy 8:3].
Matthew 4:3-4

Then Jesus told [Satan],
"Go away, Satan! For it is written:
Worship the Lord your God,
and serve only Him" [Deuteronomy 6:13].
Matthew 4:10

He turned and told Peter,
"Get behind Me, Satan! You are an offense to Me
because you're not thinking about God's concerns, but man's."
Matthew 16:23

Then the Devil left Him . . . .
Matthew 4:11

**PRAYER:**

Father, thank You for the authority Your Word gives me
to eliminate destructive influences in my life,
as well as the verses that encourage and
remind me of just how much I am loved.

# WHAT IS YOUR LOGO?

Creating a logo is vital for building a brand and successfully marketing a product. BMW, Mercedes, Acura, Infinity—they all have an emblem on the hood and trunk so that, at a glance, you can tell exactly who the maker is, then dream about owning one for yourself. When it comes to living out your faith and being part of building God's Kingdom, the ultimate goal is to live in such a way that, at a glance, others will know you're a Christian, and they'll want to follow you toward God. Bottom line, the Maker wants everyone to dream about life with Him—and for that dream to come true.

Many women who had followed Jesus from Galilee
and ministered to Him were there,
looking on from a distance.
Matthew 27:55

For we did not follow cleverly contrived myths
when we made known to you the power and coming
of our Lord Jesus Christ;
instead, we were eyewitnesses of His majesty.
II Peter 1:16

Therefore, be imitators of God,
as dearly loved children.
Ephesians 5:1

In the same way,
let your light shine before others,
so that they may see your good works and
give glory to your Father who is in heaven.
Matthew 5:16 ESV

PRAYER:

Lord, thank You for the honor and privilege of being part
of Your Kingdom and using me as a vessel for bringing
others to You. Hopefully—by Your grace—I exemplify Your
love to a lost world in a way that draws them to You.

# NO CONDEMNATION

Receiving grace from God is nothing short of a superlative gift. Extending grace to others is what we are called to do since God extends it to us. But what about receiving grace from ourselves? Oftentimes, when we fail at something, we can be harder on ourselves than anyone else we know. But God doesn't want us to live under condemnation, and that includes self-condemnation. "Therefore, no condemnation now exists for those in Christ Jesus" (Romans 8:1). Believe it, claim it, and live in the space of grace we have as followers of Christ. We are to live in freedom.

Christ has liberated us to be free.
Stand firm then and don't submit again to a yoke of slavery.
Galatians 5:1

I assure you: Anyone who hears My word and
believes Him who sent Me has eternal life
and will not come under judgment
but has passed from death to life.
John 5:24

For Moses gave us only the Law
with its rigid demands and merciless justice,
while Jesus Christ brought us loving forgiveness as well.
John 1:17 TLB

Therefore, no condemnation now exists for those
in Christ Jesus, because the Spirit's law
of life in Christ Jesus has set you free
from the law of sin and of death.
Romans 8:1-2

PRAYER:

Father, thank You for the reminder not to condemn myself—
it's a weight You lifted long ago. I believe Your Word and
want to walk in the freedom Your grace provides this day forward.

# SOME THINGS ARE WORTH REMEMBERING

Are you feeling discouraged about something? Then take time to remember. Even though the Bible is filled with stories of God's faithfulness over centuries past, you've got your own list of times and ways He's blessed your life. Begin with His gift of salvation and the day you accepted it. Remember the prayers He has answered. Recount His kindnesses to you and the grace He has shown. His love for you burns strong, His faithfulness is steadfast, and His presence is ever constant. So keep remembering what He has done and rejoice in knowing He will come through again.

These things I remember as I pour out my soul: how I used to go to the house of God under the protection of the Mighty One with shouts of joy and praise among the festive throng.
Psalm 42:4 NIV

Don't you understand even yet? Don't you remember the 5,000 I fed with five loaves, and the baskets of leftovers you picked up?
Matthew 16:9 NLT

Remember what you were in the past. At that time you were apart from Christ. . . . But now, in union with Christ Jesus you, who used to be far away, have been brought near by the blood of Christ.
Ephesians 2:11-13 GNT

I trust in Your love.
My heart is happy because You saved me.
Psalm 13:5 ICB

## PRAYER:

O Lord, when I recount the ways You've blessed
my life, my hope is renewed, and Your peace
rules in my heart once again. Thank You for Your
abundance and grace, Your mercy and love.

# SERVANT'S HEART, GRATEFUL HEART

A servant's heart is a grateful heart. How can this be? Taking meals to shut-ins illuminates your freedom to come and go as you please. Giving to families in need ignites the brevity that their situation could easily be yours. Buying toys and coats for children in less fortunate homes brings back memories of a day when others came through for you. Serving others is serving Jesus. It's being Christ's eyes for seeing those in need, and His arm for extending His compassion. The reward is a grateful heart as you realize that He reaches for You the same way you reach out to others.

Do God's will from your heart.
Serve with a good attitude, as to the Lord and not to men,
knowing that whatever good each one does . . .
he will receive this back from the Lord.
Ephesians 6:6-8


For the Son of Man came not to be cared for.
He came to care for others.
Matthew 20:28 NLV


For who is the greater,
one who reclines at table or one who serves?
Is it not the one who reclines at table?
But I am among you as the One who serves.
Luke 22:27 ESV

day

58

You will be enriched in every way
so that you can be generous on every occasion,
and through us your generosity
will result in thanksgiving to God.
II Corinthians 9:11 NIV

## PRAYER:

Father, thank You for Your supreme example of
serving others. Help me to see their needs as You do.
Help me be sensitive to how and when You want
me to move and serve in Your spirit of love.

# WHAT MATTERS MOST

It's a constant challenge to develop deep and meaningful friendships in our fast and furious society. While we try and cram more into each day, we try and cram relationships into them as well—and results can be shallow. Think of when a rock is thrown and skips across water before sinking. It flies at high speed and bounces off the surface to maintain momentum. Can you imagine Jesus teaching and performing miracles at such a pace? This is a good reminder to slow down, to be intentional, to soak in God's grace, and to focus on what's truly important, which are matters of the heart. When you do, life is so much more as it should be, and the way God intended.

On landing at Caesarea, [Paul] went up and greeted the church and went down to Antioch. And after spending some time there, he set out, traveling through one place after another in the Galatian territory and Phrygia, strengthening all the disciples.
Acts 18:22-23

I don't want to see you now just in passing, for I hope to spend some time with you, if the Lord allows.
I Corinthians 16:7

He says, "Be still, and know that I am God."
Psalm 46:10 NIV

day
9

And after [Judas and Silas] had spent some time,
they were sent off in peace by the brothers
to those who had sent them.
Acts 15:33 ESV

PRAYER:

Lord, help me to take a deep breath today and really think
about the most important things I should focus on—
things that are meaningful and lasting.
Help me to see You and touch others in a way that truly matters.

# ROYAL RESERVATIONS

When you want to reserve a venue for a future event, such as a wedding or reunion, it's common to pay a deposit to guarantee your access when the time comes to use it. The deposit proves you're serious about using the place, plus it reserves your spot on the provider's calendar. Did you know that, by God's grace, this is what Jesus does when you accept Him as Savior? He instills His Spirit inside of you as a deposit for what's to come in heaven with Him. Your reservation is secured and guaranteed . . . forever. Until your spot is filled—by you—He lives within you here on earth, giving hope and guidance until He ushers you into His grand entrance of eternity. All praise be to Him.

When you believed, you were marked in Him with a seal, the promised Holy Spirit, who is a deposit guaranteeing our inheritance until the redemption of those who are God's possession—to the praise of His glory.
Ephesians 1:13-14 NIV

Guard the good deposit that was entrusted to you—guard it with the help of the Holy Spirit who lives in us.
II Timothy 1:14 NIV

He has also sealed us and given us the Spirit as a down payment in our hearts.
II Corinthians 1:22

Now it is God who makes both us and
you stand firm in Christ. He anointed us,
set His seal of ownership on us,
and put His Spirit in our hearts as a deposit,
guaranteeing what is to come.
II Corinthians 1:21-22 NIV

PRAYER:

Father, I am so grateful for Your Spirit—
it's leading, guiding, and reserving a place
for me to be with You for always.

# HOLY RESIDENCE

You are holy—yes, holy. So stop, take a deep breath, and soak that in for a bit. You are holy, because our holy God resides in you. If you've accepted Him as your Savior and asked Him into your heart, He is in you now to love, lead, empower, comfort, strengthen, and bless according to His purpose for your life. Just as you walk into a beautiful sanctuary to worship God, His Spirit has entered you to reside and be in relationship with . . . you. It's a miracle only God can do, and it's true. You are holy.

But as the One who called you is holy,
you also are to be holy in all your conduct;
for it is written, Be holy, because I am holy.
I Peter 1:15-16

Don't you know that your body is a sanctuary
of the Holy Spirit who is in you,
whom you have from God? You are not your own,
for you were bought at a price.
Therefore glorify God in your body.
I Corinthians 6:19-20

He has saved us and called us with a holy calling,
not according to our works,
but according to His own purpose and grace.
II Timothy 1:9

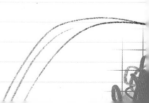

Don't you yourselves know that you are
God's sanctuary and that the Spirit of God lives in you?
... God's sanctuary is holy, and that is what you are.

I Corinthians 3:16-17

PRAYER:

Father God, the thought of being holy is humbling.
It's also honoring to know that Your Spirit is in me.
I love and cherish You, and I'm so happy to be Your child.

# HOW DO YOU SHOW GRATITUDE?

It's hard not to break into a smile when you look down and see a dog or cat showing gratitude. Dogs will wag their tail—the happier they are, the faster they wag. When they're really grateful, they pant, wag, and dance around all at the same time. When cats are grateful they rub up against you and purr. Sometimes they knead and even drool when they purr, which means they're extra glad.

So how do you show gratitude to the Father? Certainly not by wagging and drooling! Shouting, singing, laughing, and lifting prayers of praise and thanksgiving are all ways to express heartfelt gratefulness. Tearing up . . . that shows you're extra thankful. When you display any of these forms of thanksgiving, there's no doubt God has an extra-big smile looking down on you.

I will offer sacrifices in His tent with shouts of joy.
I will sing and make music to the Lord.
Psalm 27:6

Give thanks to Yahweh; proclaim His name! . . . Sing to Yahweh,
for He has done glorious things. Cry out and sing . . .
for the Holy One of Israel is among you in His greatness.
Isaiah 12:4-6

Therefore will I give thanks and praise You, O Lord,
among the nations, and sing praises to Your name.
Psalm 18:49 AMP

Be glad in the LORD and rejoice,
you righteous ones; shout for joy,
all you upright in heart.
Psalm 32:11

PRAYER:

Father, thank You that I can celebrate my love and
thanksgiving for You in a variety of ways. You make me smile,
so I love the thought of making You smile even more.

# WHOM DO YOU WORK FOR?

What's on your agenda for today? Is it full of deadlines at work or children to feed? Do the tasks ahead look momentous and hard or boring and insignificant? No matter your vocation, no matter the chore, what's most important is doing it for God. Not for your boss or spouse or neighbor, but for Jesus Himself. So praise Jesus and thank Him for the opportunity to be of use to Him—whatever that looks like. Working for God turns work into an expression of love toward the One who blesses humble hands for His service.

I count my life of no value to myself,
so that I may finish my course and the ministry
I received from the Lord Jesus,
to testify to the gospel of God's grace.
Acts 20:24

In the same way, let your light shine before men,
so that they may see your good works and
give glory to your Father in heaven.
Matthew 5:16

The Lord is my strength and my shield;
my heart trusts in Him, and I am helped.
Therefore my heart rejoices, and I praise Him with my song.
Psalm 28:7

Whatever you do, do it enthusiastically,
as something done for the Lord and not for men.
Colossians 3:23

Lord, thank You for work to do today. Thank You for purpose and
the gifts and talents I need to fulfill the plans You have for me.

# JUDGMENT-FREE ZONE

There's a national fitness center that has what they call a Judgment-Free Zone. Whoever walks through their doors to exercise is promised not to be judged by appearance, which is a relief, because our society is quick to judge—our looks, our abilities, our successes (and failures). But there's another judgment-free zone we can live in: it's the platform we hold as a child of God. He doesn't judge or condemn—instead, He loves, accepts, renews, encourages, and blesses beyond measure. We are members of His royal family for life. There's no better "zone" than that.

The earth is full of
the Lord's unfailing love.
Psalm 33:5

All the prophets testify about Him
that through His name everyone who believes
in Him will receive forgiveness of sins.
Acts 10:43

So now there is no condemnation
for those who belong to Christ Jesus.
Romans 8:1 NLT

There is deliverance from judgment
because the Prince of this world
has already been judged.
John 16:11 TLB

## PRAYER:

Father, thank You for providing peace of
mind and heart to live and rest in Your
full acceptance—just the way I am.

# THIS IS NOT YOUR HOME

Did you know your body is a tent? That's right, a tent. Tents are meant to provide short-term living spaces while you're away from home. And life on this earth is just that—a temporary place to live until you go to your heavenly home. Some tent-stays last longer than others, but eventually, each of us will pull up our stakes, collapse our poles, fold up our tent, and go home. At home, there is no sickness, no sadness, no sin—only joyful praise and worship to the almighty King of kings. It's where angels are waiting to rejoice and welcome you to the Father. Home sweet home to the Savior—how sweet that day will be.

For we know that when this tent we live in now is taken down—
when we die and leave these bodies—
we will have wonderful new bodies in heaven,
homes that will be ours forevermore,
made for us by God Himself and not by human hands.
How weary we grow of our present bodies.
That is why we look forward eagerly to the day
when we shall have heavenly bodies
that we shall put on like new clothes.
II Corinthians 5:1-2 TLB

Based on His promise,
we wait for the new heavens and a new earth,
where righteousness will dwell.
II Peter 3:13

# day 65

For we know that if our temporary,
earthly dwelling is destroyed,
we have a building from God,
an eternal dwelling in the heavens,
not made with hands.

II Corinthians 5:1

**PRAYER:**

Father, I love living in Your beautiful creation here on earth,
but I long for the day when I will be in my permanent, heavenly
home with You. I can't imagine how magnificent it will be.

# GOT PLANS?

God has a plan for your life. But chances are, you have a plan for your life too. And chances are, most days, your plan takes precedence over God's. Why? Well, because yours is an amazing plan! You have a list of exciting things you want to do and ways that you want to live—it's a wonderful plan. But . . . God has a plan for your life. Do you think His plan might be just a little bit greater than yours? Well, it is—so much so, you can't even imagine it. So, will you trust Him? Will you seek His will—His plan—with all your heart? If the answer is yes, you will never be sorry. Ever. Oh, and . . . remember to fasten your seatbelt.

Lord my God, You have done many things—
Your wonderful works and Your plans for us;
none can compare with You.
If I were to report and speak of them,
they are more than can be told.
Psalm 40:5

Now to Him who is able to do immeasurably more
than all we ask or imagine,
according to His power that is at work within us.
Ephesians 3:20 NIV

Commit your works to the Lord,
and your plans will be established.
Proverbs 16:3 NET

**66**

"For I know the plans I have for you"—
this is the LORD's declaration—
"plans for your welfare, not for disaster,
to give you a future and a hope.
Jeremiah 29:11

**PRAYER:**

Lord, it's hard to let go of my plans! But I want to—
I want to trust You enough to give my plans to You and
follow wherever You lead. Give me the courage to be, to do,
and to live Your plans for me, and in a way
that brings You all the glory.

# HOW WILL YOU SLEEP TONIGHT?

There's a pillow ad that frequently runs on TV, and it claims this pillow will give you the best night's sleep you've ever had. It's better than any other pillow on the market, and you are promised better sleep or your money back. It's true—a good pillow does make a difference in how well you sleep. But God has an even better approach to a sound slumber: a clear conscience. And the only way to have a clear conscience is to humble yourself, confess your sins to Him, and ask for His forgiveness. When you do, by His grace, you are cleansed, and the weight of sin vanishes. God then instills a supernatural peace and calm that no pillow can come close to matching. How will you sleep tonight?

People who conceal their sins will not prosper,
but if they confess and turn from them, they will receive mercy.
Proverbs 28:13 NLT

Admit your faults to one another and pray for each
other so that you may be healed. The earnest prayer of a
righteous man has great power and wonderful results.
James 5:16 TLB

You were washed, you were sanctified,
you were justified in the name of the Lord Jesus
Christ and by the Spirit of our God.
I Corinthians 6:11 NET

If we confess our sins,
He is faithful and righteous
to forgive us our sins and
to cleanse us from all unrighteousness.

I John 1:9

## PRAYER:

Father, I confess to You now that I don't confess enough!
Starting now, I humble myself and bring to You my sins.
I pray for the gift of peace—Your peace that
brings a state of complete rest for my soul.

# GOD CHOSE YOU

Are you aware that God chose you? Yes, He chose you to be in His family, imperfections and all. From billions of people in the world, He chose you for a special purpose. And when you seek Him and carry out that purpose, He has blessing above your imagination in store. Oftentimes His way is not easy, but His grace and power, love and devotion meet where you aren't able. The rewards for walking with God and glorifying Him are abundant and all-surpassing. Nothing else compares to what He has in store just for you.

He brought forth His people with joy,
His chosen ones with a joyful shout.
Psalm 105:43 NASB

If you belonged to the world,
the world would love you as its own.
However, I have chosen you out of the world,
and you don't belong to the world.
John 15:19 CEB

For He chose us in Him, before the foundation of the world,
to be holy and blameless in love before Him.
He predestined us to be adopted as sons through Jesus Christ
for Himself, according to the good pleasure of His will.
Ephesians 1:4-5 CSB

I chose you and appointed you
so that you might go and bear fruit—
fruit that will last—
and so that whatever you ask
in my name the Father will give you.
John 15:16 NIV

**PRAYER:**

Father, I am humbled to know that You chose me,
and that You have a specific purpose just for me.
Please show me, lead me, guide me so that I am right where
You want me to be, doing what You would have me to do.

# CHRIST HAS SET YOU FREE

Imagine being a little bird locked up in a cage only to sit on a perch, never to use your wings. But one day, someone carries your cage outside, lifts the door, and says, "Fly, little one! Fly as God made you to!" Oh, the wonder and excitement, the joy and the rush from that first push off the door frame and into the open sky. After flying into freedom, you wouldn't fly back into that cage again . . . or would you? So oftentimes that's what we do after God releases us from shame or whatever prison our heart was in before—we return. But freedom in Christ doesn't come with a return address—when He says free, He means free.

For the Lord is the Spirit,
and wherever the Spirit of the Lord is,
there is freedom.
II Corinthians 3:17 NLT

If you continue in My word, you really are My disciples.
You will know the truth, and the truth will set you free.
John 8:31-32

But thanks be to God, that you who were once slaves of sin
have become obedient from the heart to the standard
of teaching to which you were committed, and,
having been set free from sin,
have become slaves of righteousness.
Romans 6:17-18 RSV

Christ has set us free to live a free life.
So take your stand! Never again let anyone
put a harness of slavery on you.
Galatians 5:1 THE MESSAGE

**PRAYER:**

O God, thank You for setting me free from the weight of sin
I used to carry. My spirit is more alive than ever—
I love my life surrendered to You and You alone.

# YOU ARE ROYALTY

Medicine and technology have come so far today that you can literally get your own DNA test to discover your complete genealogy. The thought of knowing everyone you are related to is both fascinating and tempting. After all, you might be related to royalty and not even know it. But wait . . . you are! Through the genealogy of Jesus Christ, your spiritual lineage travels back as far as Father Abraham. You are in God's royal family. That means you're a saint, a princess, and a daughter of the King.

Then God brought Abram outside beneath the nighttime sky
and told him, "Look up into the heavens and count the stars
if you can. Your descendants will be like that—
too many to count!"
Genesis 15:5 TLB


If you belong to Christ,
then you are Abraham's seed,
heirs according to the promise.
Galatians 3:29


To God's church at Corinth, to those who are sanctified
in Christ Jesus and called as saints.
I Corinthians 1:2

You are no longer foreigners and strangers,
but fellow citizens with the saints,
and members of God's household,
built on the foundation of the apostles and prophets,
with Christ Jesus Himself as the cornerstone.

Ephesians 2:19-20

**PRAYER:**

Lord, I am honored and in awe of the fact that I am part of Your
royal family. Help me to fully embrace the crown of sainthood
that, by Your grace, You have given me through Your Son Jesus.

# WE ARE HIS CREATION

God's creation is so incredibly vast, human minds can't comprehend the enormity. We can process parts of it at a time, but as a whole, it's immeasurable. He not only created more stars in the heavens than we can count, He has given each one a name. There are galaxies, nebulas, planets, the earth. Earth inhabits billions of people, and, like the stars, God knows each of us by name. He even knows the number of hairs on our heads. It seems we should feel infinitely small in the bigger, overall picture of His creation, yet His love is so enormous, we actually feel special. That's because, in His sight, we are.

He has also put eternity in their hearts,
but man cannot discover the work
God has done from beginning to end.
Ecclesiastes 3:11

He counts the number of the stars; He gives names to all of them.
Our LORD is great, vast in power; His understanding is infinite.
Psalm 147:4-5

Thus says the LORD, who gives the sun for light by day and the fixed
order of the moon and the stars for light by night, who stirs up
the sea so that its waves roar—the LORD of hosts is his name.
Jeremiah 31:35 ESV

God even knows how many hairs are on your head.
Matthew 10:30 NCV

day

# 1

When I observe Your heavens,
the work of Your fingers,
the moon and the stars,
which You set in place,
what is man that You remember him,
the son of man that You look after him?
Psalm 8:3-4

## PRAYER:

Father God, it's hard to imagine that,
with the entire universe at Your fingertips,
You see me. You know me. What a gift!
Your love fills my heart to overflowing.

# THIRST FOR GOD

When the weather is scorching or you've just finished a long, hard workout, there's nothing more enjoyable and satisfying than drinking an ice cold carbonated beverage. But not long after that last swallow, thirst arises for another. And another. As in life, when you face the heat of trials or you're playing hard in the fast lane, there are many ways to comfort and satisfy—for a while. Temporary fixes are short lived. When you drink from the fountain of truth in God's Word and embrace the way He has for you, you will be deeply satisfied in the wellspring of His grace. He is the water of life and eternity.

The Lord will always lead you,
satisfy you in a parched land . . . .
You will be like a watered garden
and like a spring whose waters never run dry.
Isaiah 58:11

"I am the bread of life," Jesus told them.
"No one who comes to Me will ever be hungry,
and no one who believes in Me will ever be thirsty again."
John 6:35

Let them give thanks to the Lord for His unfailing love
and His wonderful deeds for mankind,
for He satisfies the thirsty
and fills the hungry
with good things.
Psalm 107:8–9 NIV

But whoever drinks the water that I give him will never be thirsty again. But the water that I give him will become in him a spring of water [satisfying his thirst for God] welling up [continually flowing, bubbling within him] to eternal life.

John 4:14 AMP

## PRAYER:

Father, thank You for Your fountain of love, joy, and goodness in my life. Nothing can compare to the lasting satisfaction You bring to my soul.

# FROM THE EYES
# OF A CHILD

There is a fun kids game called I Spy with My Little Eye. One child looks around and spots something, then says, "I spy with my little eye something that is . . ." and then gives a clue. Then the other kids look around and guess what it is based on the clue. Well, you can play a similar version yourself by saying, "I spy Jesus in . . ." and state something you're grateful for. It could be a hug from a child, a smile from a stranger, or an unexpected card in the mail—God is in them all. It may be a child's game, but sometimes having a child's pure and simple heart helps see through the grime of life and cast a smile on so many things there are to be glad about.

We give thanks to You, God; we give thanks to You,
for Your name is near. People tell about
Your wonderful works.
Psalm 75:1

Whatever you do, in word or in deed,
do everything in the name of the Lord Jesus,
giving thanks to God the Father through Him.
Colossians 3:17

Be filled by the Spirit . . . giving thanks always for everything
to God the Father in the name of our Lord Jesus Christ.
Ephesians 5:18, 20

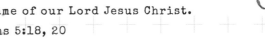

## day 73

Rejoice always!
Pray constantly.
Give thanks in everything,
for this is God's will for you
in Christ Jesus.
I Thessalonians 5:16-18

## PRAYER:

Father, when I really look and ponder on all
that I have and all the good You've done in my life,
I cannot find the words to express the depths of
my gratitude. Thank You for Your kindnesses to me!

# ROUND OF APPLAUSE

When you've worked especially hard on something, isn't it nice to be recognized and honored for your efforts? Whether working for weeks on a recital, months on a fundraiser, or years on a research project, getting a round of applause that celebrates your accomplishment brings joy to the heart. It's the same joy that blesses God's heart when you stop and offer up thanks to Him. He surrounds His children with blessing upon blessing—with new life, His creation, His provision, His faithfulness. The list is endless. Giving thanks, applauding the Savior for His daily care and love, is the very least you can do to show honor to the One who deserves it most.

Give thanks in everything; for this is God's
will for you in Christ Jesus.
I Thessalonians 5:18 CSB

Give thanks to the LORD and proclaim His greatness.
Let the whole world know what He has done.
Sing to Him; yes, sing His praises.
Tell everyone about His wonderful deeds.
I Chronicles 16:8-9 NLT

Give thanks to the LORD, call on His name;
proclaim His deeds among the peoples.
Sing to Him, sing praise to Him;
tell about all His wondrous works! Honor His holy name;
let the hearts of those who seek the LORD rejoice.
Psalm 105:1-3 CSB

# day 74

Whoever presents
a thank-offering honors Me.
Psalm 50:23 NET

## PRAYER:

Father, thank You from my heart
for Your goodness in my life.
I appreciate Your special touches throughout
each day, both small and big ones.
You fill my heart with joy and gladness
in ways no one else can. I love You.

# REMEMBRANCE DAY

Consider making today a Remembrance Day. Take a few moments and think back on a time, a place, or a person that was a positive experience or influence in your life. Consider writing a letter expressing gratitude for the memory—the more details the better. Being intentional about expressing thanks, whether face-to-face or on paper, blesses the recipient and sets your mind and mood into one that exudes happiness and joy. The more joy you have, the more love you show. The more love you show, the more God is glorified. If, in the end, God is glorified, maybe every day should be a Remembrance Day.

I thank my God every time I remember you.
Philippians 1:3 NIV

I never stop giving thanks for you
as I remember you in my prayers.
Ephesians 1:16

I always thank my God for you because of God's grace
given to you in Christ Jesus,
that by Him you were enriched in everything—
in all speech and all knowledge.
I Corinthians 1:4-5

# 75

Dear brothers and sisters,
we can't help but thank God for you,
because your faith is flourishing and
your love for one another is growing.
II Thessalonians 1:3 NLT

**PRAYER:**

Father, thank You for crossing my paths with so many people
who have encouraged and blessed me.
Lead my thoughts to all You would have me reach
out to and, hopefully, bless them in return.

# OPEN-DOOR POLICY

It's not uncommon for a CEO of a company to have a large and beautiful office that's been professionally decorated, has a gorgeous view, and has a door . . . that's closed. Of course, a closed door means "Do not disturb. I am busy. What I'm doing is more important and urgent than talking to you." A closed door isn't meant to offend or hurt your feelings—CEOs are very important, busy people. But the only way to open their door is by making an appointment.

Isn't it wonderful that the CEO of the universe has an open-door policy? It's always open. Always. He wants you to enter His presence as often as you can and speak for as long as you like. He is never too busy for you.

Know that the Lord has set apart
the faithful for Himself;
the Lord will hear when I call to Him.
Psalm 4:3 CSB

For we do not have a high priest
who is unable to sympathize with our weaknesses,
but One who has been tested in every way as we are,
yet without sin. Therefore let us approach
the throne of grace with boldness,
so that we may receive mercy and
find grace to help us at the proper time.
Hebrews 4:15-16

Call to Me and come and pray to Me,
and I will listen to you.
You will seek Me and find Me
when you search for Me
with all your heart.
Jeremiah 29:12-13

## PRAYER:

Father, by Your abundant grace, thank You for removing
all barriers so I'm able to approach You at any time.
Thank You for being available and interested in what
I have to say no matter the time of day or night.

# TALKING TO GOD

Oftentimes prayer can be a mystery, especially to new Christians. The disciples, who walked with Jesus, were even confused about how to pray, so they finally asked Him how (Luke 11:1). But prayer is simple: it is merely opening your heart and speaking freely to God . . . about anything. Nothing is off limits. He wants you to give prayer your all. It's your time to praise, thank, petition, confess, cry out, intercede, and even rest in God's presence. He not only listens to every word, He speaks back—it's literally a conversation with the King of all kings. By His grace, you have a supernatural way to stay connected and attuned to the Father, and He to you. Thank God for the gift of prayer.

The Lord has heard my supplication;
the Lord will receive my prayer.
Psalm 6:9 NKJV

You will call to Me and come and pray to Me,
and I will listen to you.
You will seek Me and find Me when you
search for Me with all your heart.
Jeremiah 29:12–13

[Jesus] was praying in a certain place,
and when He finished,
one of His disciples said to Him,
"Lord, teach us to pray."
Luke 11:1

But when you pray,
go into your room and shut the door
and pray to your Father who is in secret.
And your Father who sees in secret
will reward you.
Matthew 6:6 ESV

PRAYER:

Father, to know that I can speak to You any time day or night is
a gift. I have a lot to say, so I open my heart to You now . . .

# PURE AND HOLY LOVE

When you look at and think on the word *sinner*, there is no good or just thought to put with it—sin is all that is bad. And yet, while all of humanity was full of sin, God in all His humility, goodness, and love poured down His holy oil of grace—Jesus—to remove sin's effects from all who receive Him. That is pure love.

"It is an unseemly sight to see God humbling Himself and man exalting himself; to see a humble Savior and a proud sinner."

—THOMAS WATSON

For I passed on to you as most important
what I also received: that Christ died
for our sins according to the Scriptures . . . .
I Corinthians 15:3

For while we were still helpless,
at the right time, Christ died for the ungodly.
Romans 5:6 CSB

He humbled Himself
by becoming obedient to the point of death—
even to death on a cross.
Philippians 2:8

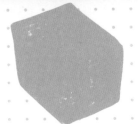

But God demonstrates His own love for us in this:
While we were still sinners, Christ died for us.

Romans 5:8 NIV

PRAYER:

Lord, thank You for dying for me—
before I even knew You and loved You.
That is the deepest form of love I've ever known.
I am grateful from the core of my heart. I love You.

# THE OFFERING OF PRAYER

Don't you love to walk into a kitchen and smell the aroma of fresh brewed coffee? And what about fresh baked bread? Or bacon?! Yes, these scents are very pleasing and comforting down to the core. But did you know that your prayers are a sweet-smelling aroma to God? Praying unlocks sincerity and praise from your heart, and He is delighted to receive them. He loves fellowship with you and is waiting to bless you during times of devotion and stillness with Him. Your authentic and genuine prayers are an offering heard by a Father in heaven who loves you very much. So pray about everything—lift up your praise, your heartfelt petitions, and songs of worship to Him.

The Lord said to him, "I have heard your prayer
which you have prayed to Me.
I have set apart this house you have built
by putting My name there forever.
My eyes and My heart will be there always."
I Kings 9:3 NLV

During those days [Jesus] went out to the mountain
to pray and spent all night in prayer to God.
Luke 6:12

The angel told [Cornelius],
"Your prayers and your acts of charity have come up
as a memorial offering before God."
Acts 10:4

day

79

May my prayer be set before You as incense,
the raising of my hands as the evening offering.
Psalm 141:2

PRAYER:

Lord, I love You, praise You,
and thank You for hearing my prayers and
for receiving mine now, today, and every day.

# FROM ONE PARENT TO ANOTHER

If you're a mom, you've experienced how the big-picture view of motherhood overflows your heart to no end. To have children and a family to call your own, to enjoy first smiles, first words, first steps—nothing compares. Then there is the up-close, day-to-day view. The endless laundry, dried oatmeal, runny noses, sleepless nights—it is overwhelming. The good news is knowing that both views are held together with a strength far greater than your own. God smiles in the wonder and has compassion through the challenges. His wisdom, grace, and helping hands are sandwiched between the birth dates and graduation dates. From one Parent to another, He has you in His arms to hold you up and see you through. You are not alone, thanks be to God.

As a father has compassion on His children,
so the Lord has compassion on His faithful followers.
Psalm 103:13 NET

Children are a gift from the Lord;
they are a reward from Him.
Psalm 127:3 NLT

The Spirit helps us in our weakness.
Romans 8:26 NIV

My grace is all you need.
My power works best in weakness.
II Corinthians 12:9 NLT

## PRAYER:

Father, thank You for being with me on this incredible journey of motherhood. I'm so grateful for the days when I'm able to keep up and soak in the joys it brings. And I thank You that on the days when I am weak, You hold me up and carry me through.

# THE FINAL SAY

Who doesn't like having the final say about something? It brings a feeling of authority and control that we, as humans, love to possess. The very best final say you ever had went into effect the day you accepted Christ as your Savior. When you entered into relationship with Him, you agreed that He could have the final say over your life. And He says He has a purpose and a plan for you . . . You can triumph over strongholds . . . . You have access to His power and even His mind . . . You will spend eternity with Him. Through His love and by His grace, you will live in His presence, both now and forever. That's His final say.

For WHO HAS KNOWN THE MIND
*and* PURPOSES OF THE LORD,
SO AS TO INSTRUCT HIM?
But we have the mind of Christ
[to be guided by His thoughts and purposes].
I Corinthians 2:16 AMP

I call to God Most High,
to God who fulfills His purpose for me.
Psalm 57:2

The LORD has made everything
for its own purpose.
Proverbs 16:4 AMP

There is no longer any room for doubt,
and we can tell others that salvation is ours,
for there is no question that
He will do what He says.
Hebrews 10:23 TLB

PRAYER:

Father God, thank You for the security
in knowing that You are in control.
Thank You for empowering me to live
a victorious life under the constant
covering of Your love and grace.

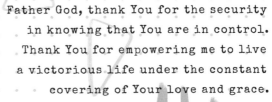

# APPROACHING GOD'S THRONE

Since Old Testament times, there have been royal thrones where kings and queens have sat and ruled their domain. They were fancy seats where an everyday man or woman could approach his or her majesty to speak about a matter of concern or face a looming judgment. The regulations and traditions for approaching a throne were so numerous, it's enough to turn your stomach and retreat. But there is a throne that's different and above all others—God's. It is a throne of grace, and we, as believers, can approach it boldly. It's where we are protected from judgment and covered by His love. The Majesty invites anyone to approach and be greeted with open arms.

Righteousness and justice are the foundation of Your throne;
faithful love and truth go before You.
Psalm 89:14

Seek the Lord while He may be found;
call to Him while He is near.
Isaiah 55:6

The LORD is near all who call out to Him, all who call out to Him with integrity. He fulfills the desires of those who fear Him; He hears their cry for help and saves them.
Psalm 145:18-19

## day 82

Therefore let us approach
the throne of grace with boldness,
so that we may receive mercy and
find grace to help us at the proper time.

Hebrews 4:16

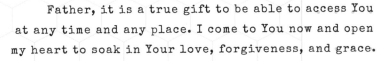

**PRAYER:**

Father, it is a true gift to be able to access You
at any time and any place. I come to You now and open
my heart to soak in Your love, forgiveness, and grace.

# THANKSGIVING DAY

Every year since 1621, Americans have planned and gathered together for one day for a single purpose: to give thanks. It's a day to ponder, remember, celebrate, break bread, and share stories of God's abundance, both big and small. Whether for His blessing of provision, victory in battle, or the very gift of life, giving thanks has been an annual tradition since the founding of this country. Likewise, since the founding of your salvation—the day you came to accept Jesus as Savior—every day is cause to lift up your hands in praise and speak gratitude from your heart. You can shout out loud or whisper softly, just remember to let the words *Thank You* be said.

David's song of thanksgiving: The Lord is my rock, my
fortress, and my deliverer, my God, my mountain where I seek
refuge. My shield, the horn of my salvation, my stronghold,
my refuge, and my Savior, You save me from violence.
II Samuel 22:2-3

O Lord, I will praise You with all my heart and tell
everyone about the marvelous things You do.
Psalm 9:1 TLB

Give thanks to the Lord, for He is good;
His faithful love endures forever.
Psalm 107:1

Then say, "Save us, O God of our salvation;
Gather us together and rescue us from the nations,
That we may give thanks to Your holy name,
And glory in Your praise."
I Chronicles 16:35 AMP

day 83

You turned my lament into dancing;
You removed my sackcloth
and clothed me with gladness,
so that I can sing to You and not be silent.
LORD my God, I will praise You forever.
Psalm 30:11-12

PRAYER:

Father, THANK YOU. Thank You for Your perfect provision and love.
For armor to fight the enemy, and for Your Word to stand in truth.
Most of all, for Your kindness and forgiveness of my sins. Thank You.

# BE KIND

Cultivating kindness is not easy. You can leave for work thinking, *Today, I'm going to be kind to others*. Then you are cut off in traffic, your boss takes credit for one of your ideas, and a client snaps a foul comment your way. So much for being kind! All your well-intended responses turn into getting defensive and stewing. It's a constant battle to resist rudeness and not give in to snarling back. But you are called—even commanded—to show love and kindness to your neighbor. Especially to the mean and thoughtless ones. It's what sets your testimony of "Christ in you" apart from the rest of humanity. It's putting God's grace into action through you. It's not easy, but by His power, it is possible.

Do not be conquered by evil,
but conquer evil with good.
Romans 12:21

Don't say, "I'll do to him what he did to me;
I'll repay the man for what he has done."
Proverbs 24:29

To love God with all your heart and mind and strength
is very important. So is loving your neighbor
as you love yourself. These things are more important
than all burnt offerings and sacrifices.
Mark 12:33 NIRV

Be kind and compassionate to one another,
forgiving one another, just as God
also forgave you in Christ.
Ephesians 4:32

PRAYER:

Father, help me to live out kindness today. I know it's Your way of
disarming, disrobing, and dismantling the enemy's ugliness and
letting Your light and love shine through. To You be the glory.

# NOT LOOKING FOR PERFECT

Have you ever had a spiritual setback, wandered from the faith, or blown your witness as a believer? If you have, then you aren't alone—any Christian who's honest will raise their hand and say, "I have." You're also not alone in your struggle of getting back on your feet and regaining solid ground. God is there and not to scold—He doesn't point a finger and say, "I told you so." He listens to your heartfelt outpourings, cleans your wounds, and directs you back on His path. He isn't looking for perfect, He's looking for a humble and willing heart. So if that's where you are, accept the covering of His grace, and believe Him when He says, "I love you," because He does.

When you are in distress and all these things have happened
to you, in the future you will return to the LORD your God
and obey him. He will not leave you . . .
because the LORD your God is a compassionate God.
Deuteronomy 4:30-31 CSB

The LORD is waiting to show you mercy, and is rising
up to show you compassion, for the LORD is a just
God. All who wait patiently for Him are happy.
Isaiah 30:18

He forgives all your sin; He heals all your
diseases. He redeems your life from the Pit; He
crowns you with faithful love and compassion.
Psalm 103:3-4

day 85

The LORD is gracious and compassionate,
slow to anger and great in faithful love.
Psalm 145:8

**PRAYER:**

O Lord, thank You for Your patience and compassion,
and most of all, for not giving up on me.
I am so grateful I can run to You again and again
and know You are there for me.
You are my God, and You are so good.

# WHEN GOD CALLS

When God calls you to do something big, it's natural to think, *Oh, I'm not qualified to do that!* But God, in His sovereignty, doesn't judge your qualifications based on experience or education—He looks at your willingness and reliance on Him. You've probably noticed that He often nudges, sometimes even pushes toward dreams and roles far above what you would think for yourself. But figuring out how to accomplish a God-dream isn't your job—He's already got the details worked out. Your job is to show up and take the first step, so He can reveal them to you. There isn't anything He asks you to do alone—His grace covers and carries. Where you can't, He can and will.

I will boast all the more gladly of my weaknesses,
so that the power of Christ may rest upon me.
II Corinthians 12:9 ESV

The members of the council were amazed when they saw
the boldness of Peter and John, for they could see that
they were ordinary men with no special training in the Scriptures.
They also recognized them as men who had been with Jesus.
Acts 4:13 NLT

"My grace is sufficient for you, for power is perfected in weakness."
Therefore, I will most gladly boast all the more
about my weaknesses, so that Christ's power may reside in me.
II Corinthians 12:9

# day 86

Now to Him who is able to do above
and beyond all that we ask or think
according to the power that works in us.

Ephesians 3:20

PRAYER:

Father, forgive me for looking to my own sufficiency instead of Yours.
I look to You now for Your supernatural guidance, power,
and strength to walk this life journey I'm on.

# THE SACRIFICE OF PRAISE

Just what is a sacrifice of praise? After all, to sacrifice means to give something to a point of discomfort, so how can it be a discomfort to praise God? Well, when life has given you a gut punch; when you're faced with mounting troubles with no simple solutions; when you're not even sure where God is, giving praise goes against your mood and emotions. It becomes a sacrifice because it's hard to put "self" aside for a time—especially during the difficult ones—and give God the praise He still deserves. He is over your life. He's got you in His hand. Give Him the sacrifice of praise for His faithfulness and for the "ultimate sacrifice" His Son made to pave your road to eternity with Him.

I will sacrifice a freewill offering to You.
I will praise Your name, Yahweh, because it is good.
For He has delivered me from every trouble.
Psalm 54:6-7

Keep your minds on whatever is true, pure, right, holy,
friendly, and proper. Don't ever stop thinking
about what is truly worthwhile and worthy of praise.
Philippians 4:8 CEV

I will praise the Lord at all times;
His praise will always be on my lips.
I will boast in the Lord; the humble will hear and be glad.
Proclaim Yahweh's greatness with me;
let us exalt His name together.
Psalm 34:1-3

Therefore, let us offer through Jesus
a continual sacrifice of praise to God,
proclaiming our allegiance to His name.

Hebrews 13:15 NLT

Father, I ascribe to You the glory due Your name;
I worship You in the splendor of Your holiness (Psalm 29:2).
You are all-powerful, all that is wonderful, and filled
with beauty beyond compare. I love You and lift up my heart
filled with thanksgiving and praise for You this day.

# TRUTH OR LIES?

There is a constant battle that rages every moment of your day: it's called Truth vs. Lies. The battle started in the garden of Eden, and it continues full bore today. The enemy is forever trying to get your eyes off Jesus and the love He has for you and, instead, put your focus on temporal idols of pleasure that lead to emptiness and destruction. These lies are cunning and convincing, and they're meant to distract and destroy. But when you stay reliant on God's Word and follow the leading of His Spirit, He alerts you to deception. By His grace and power, you will know what is real and true, and what isn't. It's a battle you can win every day without fail.

> For the LORD gives wisdom;
> from His mouth come knowledge
> and understanding.
> Proverbs 2:6

> And we know that the Son of God has come
> and has given us understanding
> so that we may know the true One.
> I John 5:20

> The Spirit shows what is true and will come
> and guide you into the full truth.
> John 16:13 CEV

day

88

We are from God. ...
From this we know the Spirit of
truth and the spirit of deception.

I John 4:6

## PRAYER:

Lord, I am bombarded every day by the enemy
trying to get my eyes off of You, Your provision,
and Your love. By Your Spirit within me, I claim the clarity
to see his attempts for what they are and the power
to remain steadfast and strong in my faith in You.

# MAKING WISE DECISIONS

Decisions . . . So many are made from day to day. Many are small with no long-term significance. Others, well . . . making a wrong or careless one can bring a lot of hardship into your life and take you further away from where God wants you to be. When faced with momentous decisions, it's good to seek the counsel of trusted friends who know you and have past experience to keep you from making the same mistakes he or she made. But there is One who knows you better than anyone and can advise based on actually knowing the future, and that is God Himself. He's the One who planned your future and is orchestrating the details for it now. So remember to seek the highest counsel possible, and then trust it. By His grace in your life, He will lead and guide to where and what He wants you to do.

He guides me along right paths,
bringing honor to His name.
Psalm 23:3 NLT

We may think we know what is right,
but the Lord is the judge of our motives.
Share your plans with the Lord, and you will succeed.
Proverbs 16:2–3 CEV

I will lead the blind by a way they did not know;
I will guide them on paths they have not known.
I will turn darkness to light in front of them
and rough places into level ground.
Isaiah 42:16

"For I know the plans I have for you"—
this is the LORD's declaration—
"plans for your welfare, not for disaster,
to give you a future and a hope."

Jeremiah 29:11

## PRAYER:

Lord, sometimes it is so hard to hear You and
know what You want me to do and where You want
me to go. But that is what I want—to fulfill
Your plans for my life. I will continue
to seek You with all my heart and wait until
I know deep within before making decisions.

# SOLDIERS FOR CHRIST

One very good "politically correct" thing to do in this day is thank a veteran for his or her service. They've willingly put their very lives at risk so we can live free. But did you know that fellow Christians are veterans too? Yes, we are soldiers for Christ, fighting on front lines on behalf of God, His Kingdom, and one another. Through fasting and prayer, sacrifice of time, giving of resources, and sharing the gospel, we are interlocking arms and warring step-by-step against an unseen enemy who is lurking and roaming to destroy whomever he can. So thank your fellow followers of Jesus. Encouragement, camaraderie, shared purpose of goal, and unity in Christ are what keep us together and strong to the end.

Simon, Simon, look out! Satan has asked to sift you like wheat. But I have prayed for you that your faith may not fail. And you, when you have turned back, strengthen your brothers.
Luke 22:31-32

May you be strengthened with all power, according to His glorious might, for all endurance and patience, with joy giving thanks to the Father, Who has enabled you to share in the saints' inheritance in the light.
Colossians 1:11-12

Admit your faults to one another and pray for each other so that you may be healed. The earnest prayer of a righteous man has great power and wonderful results.
James 5:16 TLB

For our battle
is not against flesh and blood,
but against the rulers,
against the authorities,
against the world powers of this darkness,
against the spiritual forces
of evil in the heavens.
Ephesians 6:12

## PRAYER:

Father, thank You for this reminder
that my fellow Christians and I are in a daily battle—together.
We are not meant to do battle alone—there is great strength
in numbers. Thank You for the power we have through prayer
and extending Your love and help toward one another.

# WE ARE HIS SHEEP

Sheep are, well, stupid. They frighten over the smallest things and, without constant watch, they wander aimlessly, get into trouble, or get attacked and eaten by predators. Isn't it amazing that Jesus likens us to them? It's humbling, to say the least. Human intellect may be scores above a sheep's, but compared to God's, ours is minuscule. It's a wonder how we can think so highly of ourselves. Yet, with patience and a lot of grace, God cares for us all—the sheep in His family—as though we were royalty. That is love.

I wander like a lost sheep; seek Your servant,
for I do not forget Your commands.
Psalm 119:176

God led His people out like sheep
and He guided them like a flock through the desert.
Psalm 78:52 NCV

We all, like sheep, have gone astray,
each of us has turned to our own way;
and the Lord has laid on him the iniquity of us all.
Isaiah 53:6 NIV

If a man has a hundred sheep, and one of them has gone astray,
does he not leave the ninety-nine on the mountains
and go in search of the one that went astray?
Matthew 8:12 ESV

As [Jesus] stepped ashore, He saw a huge crowd and had compassion on them, because they were like sheep without a shepherd. Then He began to teach them many things.

Mark 6:34

PRAYER:

Father, forgive me for the days
I think more highly of myself than I should,
and for Your grace that covers all my wandering.
You are my Shepherd—oh, how I need You.

# LOOK FROM WHERE YOU'VE COME

Take a moment to think back over the years and compare your spiritual maturity then to today's. Do you flash through a series of events that have brought you closer to God? Perhaps you're stronger in faith because of a certain trial. Do things that bothered you then have the same effect or are you better at sluffing them off? It's good to look back to see from where you've come. Not to dwell, but to remember God's touching points of grace and to celebrate His faithfulness along your life's journey. Prayers that were answered, fears that were faced—they all account for a growing intimacy with the Savior and feed hope for the future to come.

Do not remember the sins of my youth or my acts of rebellion;
in keeping with Your faithful love,
remember me because of Your goodness, LORD.
The LORD is good and upright;
therefore He shows sinners the way.
Psalm 25:7–8

Remember the wondrous works He has done,
all His marvelous works, and the justice he declared.
Psalm 105:5 CEV

Remember what happened long ago, for I am God,
and there is no other; I am God,
and no one is like Me.
Isaiah 46:9

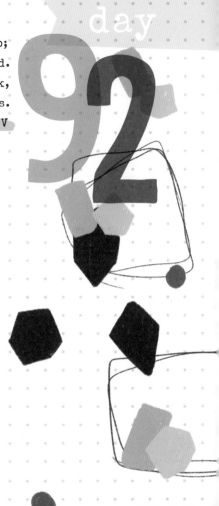

I will remember the works of the Lord;
Surely I will remember Your wonders of old.
I will also meditate on all Your work,
And talk of Your deeds.
Psalm 77:11-12 NKJV

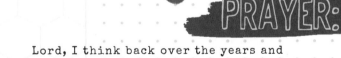

PRAYER:

Lord, I think back over the years and
how far You've brought me and how much
I've changed. I think of trials that were
difficult, yet they have grown my faith and
character and given me hope for what You'll
do in my future. I am so very grateful.

# GOD FORGETS

Don't forget!—two words we say when we're about to give a second chance to someone who's hurt us. It could be another chance at friendship, a working relationship, a marriage, or parenting a rebel. Even after they've apologized, the mind says, *Don't forget what they did.* Thankfully, this is the opposite of God's response to us. When we seek His forgiveness, by His grace, He does forget. There is no reminding and holding over our heads. It's a concept that's hard to grasp, but it's true. We are reconciled to Him and free of shame. The slate is clean. Thanks be to God.

I [Paul] do not consider myself to have taken hold of it.
But one thing I do: Forgetting what is behind
and reaching forward to what is ahead . . .
Philippians 3:13

Therefore, if anyone is in Christ,
he is a new creation;
old things have passed away,
and look, new things have come.
II Corinthians 5:17

The Lord our God is compassionate and forgiving,
even though we have rebelled against Him.
Daniel 9:9 NET

For I will forgive their wrongdoing
and never again remember their sin.

Jeremiah 31:34

## PRAYER:

Father, I am so glad You forget past sin.
Now help me not only to overlook the offense of others'
wrongdoings toward me, but mine toward You as well.

# YOU ARE WHAT YOU THINK

You've heard the saying "You are what you eat." It's true—whatever you put in your mouth gets digested and used to fuel your body. If you eat junk food, well . . . But if you eat nutritious meals, your body reflects optimal health. The same is true about what you put in your mind. Whatever you read, watch, listen to, or think about provides fuel for either optimism and power or fruitless folly and repression. Those are strong words, but song lyrics, movies, Facebook posts, and books that don't point to Christ influence the mind to be void of hope and miss out on true fulfillment. If food for thought isn't supernatural, it's superficial. May His peace, hope, and grace dwell and abide in your mind today and every day for an optimal life.

Whatever is true, whatever is honorable, whatever is just, whatever is pure, whatever is lovely, whatever is commendable—if there is any moral excellence and if there is any praise—dwell on these things.
Philippians 4:8

[Jesus] said, "I have food to eat that you don't know about. . . . My food is to do the will of Him who sent Me and to finish His work," Jesus told them.
John 4:32, 34

Set your minds on what is above, not on what is on the earth.
Colossians 3:2

day

94

The weapons of our warfare are not worldly,
but are powerful through God for the demolition
of strongholds. We demolish arguments and
every high-minded thing that is raised up
against the knowledge of God,
taking every thought captive to obey Christ.
II Corinthians 10:4-5

## PRAYER:

Lord, help me to dwell on You throughout this day.
Help me to guard what I watch, listen to, and think about,
so I can remain focused on the life and
truth that is only found in You.

# STRENGTH IN TRUST

Eagles are no less than stunning and majestic birds in God's creation. Their wingspan can get up to seven and a half feet and they can glide at altitudes of ten thousand feet for hours. They do this by finding wind thermals that literally carry them for miles so they're able to save energy and soar for very long distances. Likewise, when you trust in the Lord, your spirit gets swept up in His spiritual thermal that carries you above any mountain you're climbing or through whatever valley you're crawling in. So abide in Him and rest in His grace. You will see a breathtaking view of just how magnificent and swift His love is for you.

My grace is sufficient for you,
for My power is made perfect in weakness.
II Corinthians 12:9 NIV

He gives power to the tired and worn out,
and strength to the weak.
Isaiah 40:29 TLB

The Lord is my strength and my shield;
my heart trusts in Him, and I am helped.
Therefore my heart rejoices,
and I praise Him with my song.
Psalm 28:7

Those who trust in the LORD
will find new strength.
They will soar high on wings like eagles.
They will run and not grow weary.
They will walk and not faint.

Isaiah 40:31 NLT

**PRAYER:**

O Lord, I trust in You and rest in Your grace.
I look to You with complete abandon that Your strength
will lift me up and sustain me through
whatever I am facing.

# GRAFTED ONTO CHRIST

When you accepted Christ as Savior, you became grafted onto the vine of Jesus. Thinking on that, what kind of branch are you now? Would you be small with little buds ready to pop open? Would you be more mature, covered with vibrant leaves and pockets of lush fruit? Are you bruised from being pruned of dead twigs or disease? Whatever kind of branch you are—wherever you are in your walk with God—you're alive and being lovingly tended to by the Master Gardener. Sometimes it hurts, but only for the betterment of your growth. In His care, you are blossoming and growing into exactly who He wants you to be.

Remain in Me, and I in you.
Just as a branch is unable to produce fruit by itself
unless it remains on the vine,
so neither can you unless you remain in Me.
John 15:4

If you do boast and feel superior,
remember that it is not you who supports the root,
but the root that supports you.
Romans 11:18 AMP

If anyone does not remain in Me,
he is thrown aside like a branch and he withers.
John 15:6

I am the true vine,
and My Father is the vineyard keeper.
Every branch in Me that does not produce fruit
He removes, and He prunes every branch
that produces fruit so that
it will produce more fruit.
John 15:1-2

Father, I love You for taking the care and time for shaping
and pruning my life so I will be of strong character and
can fulfill the eternal purposes You have for me.

# PRESSURES OF LIFE

Herbs and Christians have a lot in common. The harder they are pressed, the more aroma, flavor, and character are released. Living under pressure is not easy—our first response is to avoid discomfort, not ride with it. But oftentimes God allows difficulties not only to bring us closer to Him, but to see His grace and love at work in the trenches of our hearts. They are the times that test our faith and challenge us to transport what we think about God in our heads into the application of our testimony from our hearts. And through this process, we hopefully become a pleasing scent to both God and others.

Everyone can see that the glorious power within must be from God
and is not our own. We are pressed on every side by troubles,
but not crushed and broken. We are perplexed because
we don't know why things happen as they do,
but we don't give up and quit.
II Corinthians 4:7-8 TLB

Consider it a great joy, my brothers,
whenever you experience various trials,
knowing that the testing of your faith produces endurance.
James 1:2-3

Therefore we do not lose heart. Though outwardly we are
wasting away, yet inwardly we are being renewed day by day.
For our light and momentary troubles are achieving
for us an eternal glory that far outweighs them all.
II Corinthians 4:16-17 NIV

You rejoice in this,
though now for a short time
you have had to struggle in various trials
so that the genuineness of your faith—
more valuable than gold, which perishes though
refined by fire—may result in praise, glory,
and honor at the revelation of Jesus Christ.

I Peter 1:6-7

**PRAYER:**

Father, facing and working through
my struggles is not what I want to do,
but I know I must in order to be a
sincere testimony of Your grace and
power for others. Be with me now to help
and guide, to support and comfort in
this growth process called trials.

# BURNING LOVE

When you've just come in from the cold, it's natural to pile on extra layers—thick socks, flannel PJs, a down-filled duvet—to get warm. But if you've been exposed a long time, it takes more—like sitting by a blazing fire—to get warm deep down to the core.

Likewise, it takes more to get to the root of hearts when ministering to the lost. They've been exposed to extreme and harmful elements so long that offering layers of surfacy smiles, reaching with empty hands, or praying eloquent but superficial words only touches their stone lining. To penetrate and permeate with the divine touch of Christ, there's got to be a genuine, burning flame of love. No crux of the soul can resist that of a true and sincere outpouring of God's healing balm of grace to reconcile and restore.

If I speak human or angelic languages but do not have love,
I am a sounding gong or a clanging cymbal.
If I have the gift of prophecy and understand all mysteries
and all knowledge, and if I have all faith
so that I can move mountains but do not have love, I am nothing.
And if I donate all my goods to feed the poor,
and if I give my body in order to boast but do not have love,
I gain nothing.
I Corinthians 13:1-3

Fan into flame the gift of God,
which is in you through the laying on of my hands.
II Timothy 1:6 NIV

And I know it is far more important
to love [God] with all my heart and understanding
and strength, and to love others as myself,
than to offer all kinds of sacrifices
on the altar of the Temple.
Mark 12:33 TLB

## PRAYER:

Father, just thinking of the times Your flame of love
has melted away the bitterness of my heart causes an
outpouring of thanksgiving. Help me to be real and true
in loving others, so they will know of Your love too.

# GOD IS OVER ALL

News headlines flash before us just about everywhere we look—and we don't have to look too far. From phone alerts to the TV to the radio, every day is full of troubling news that promotes fear, evil, and chaos. The good news is, God is over all. He is over all the earth and the happenings all around, and . . . He is in control. His ways are not our ways—they are sovereign and beyond our comprehension. And He is all-knowing, all-powerful, and greater than any catastrophe we are facing. What comfort and peace this brings. We may not understand what He's doing or why, but we can sing a song of praise and glory, because He does.

Yahweh does whatever He pleases in heaven and on earth,
in the seas and all the depths.
He causes the clouds to rise from the ends of the earth.
He makes lightning for the rain
and brings the wind from His storehouses.
Psalm 135:6-7

God is greater than our conscience,
and He knows all things.
I John 3:20

Yours, Lord, is the greatness and the power and
the glory and the splendor and the majesty,
for everything in the heavens and on earth belongs to You.
Yours, Lord, is the kingdom,
and You are exalted as head over all.
I Chronicles 29:11

day

# 99

Sing a song of wisdom,
for God is King of all the earth.

Psalm 47:7

PRAYER:

Father, what a relief to know that You are over all the earth.
Help me to remember that You are in control.
I wouldn't want it any other way.

# KEYS TO A TRANQUIL LIFE

Gratitude and grace—two key ingredients for a tranquil life of godliness and dignity. Who doesn't want that? Gratitude forged in prayer releases the power of God's grace under which we can dwell every day. It's a state of being that's only attained through faith that God is who He says He is. His grace is found in trusting that He'll do what He said He'll do—and that is to empower us while on this earth and build us up for eternal life in His splendor. Praise be to God for His kindness and mercy, joy and grace. To Him be the glory!

I urge that petitions, prayers, intercessions,
and thanksgivings be made for everyone,
for kings and all those who are in authority,
so that we may lead a tranquil and
quiet life in all godliness and dignity.
This is good, and it pleases God our Savior.
I Timothy 2:1-3

Be thankful. Let the message about
the Messiah dwell richly among you,
teaching and admonishing one another in all wisdom,
and singing psalms, hymns, and spiritual songs,
with gratitude in your hearts to God.
Colossians 3:15-16

And God is able to make every grace overflow to you,
so that in every way, always having everything you need,
you may excel in every good work.
II Corinthians 9:8

And now I commit you to God and
to the message of His grace,
which is able to build you up and
to give you an inheritance
among all who are sanctified.
Acts 20:32

## PRAYER:

Father, my heart is filled with gratitude for Your grace
that encompasses and fills my life each day.
You are faithful and mighty to act and to will
Your never-ending goodness and love for me to enjoy.
Thank You from the very core of my heart.

# About the Authors

**Shanna Noel** lives in Washington State with her husband of eighteen years, Jonathan, and their two daughters, Jaden (16) and Addison (11). When they aren't covered in paint and Bible journaling, they are working on reclaimed projects around the house or catching up on the latest movie.

Shanna is the founder and owner of *Illustrated Faith* and the Bible-journaling community, and stands in awe at what God is doing in their creative community!

**Lisa Stilwell** is a twenty-year veteran in corporate Christian publishing, and now has the joy of working freelance for myriad sources, including the wonderful team at DaySpring. She loves the adventure of helping authors reach deeper into their hearts and sharing the wonder and power of God with others. She also has a special compassion for caregivers, since she is one herself to her husband who has Parkinson's. Living with the challenges of neurological disease has brought a deeper reliance on God for His strength, provision, and grace—a way of life she wouldn't trade for anything.

When Lisa is not writing, editing, or spending time with her husband, you'll find her hiking to waterfalls, grilling on her back patio, watching old movies, or FaceTiming with her grandchildren. She can be reached at LoadStoneLiterary.com.

## Also Available

In her devotional journal, *100 Days of Bible Promises*, author Shanna Noel prompts you to dive into God's unwavering truth, with topics such as freedom, comfort, rest, and peace. For 100 days, you'll receive a featured Scripture, devotion, prayer, along with space for doodling, journaling, writing notes, or any other forms of creative expression. Take time to listen to the whispering voice of God, pray and reflect on His steadfast promises and allow Him to change your life. God's promises are power for living!

Available at **dayspring.com**
as well as several retail stores near you.

## More Resources

Bible journaling has become a tremendously popular new way to connect with Scripture in a creative way by combining faith and art. To learn more about Shanna Noel and the Bible Journaling movement, visit **dayspring.com/biblejournaling** today!

LIVE YOUR FAITH

*Dear Friend,*

This book was prayerfully crafted with you, the reader, in mind—every word, every sentence, every page—was thoughtfully written, designed, and packaged to encourage you...right where you are this very moment. At DaySpring, our vision is to see every person experience the life-changing message of God's love. So, as we worked through rough drafts, design changes, edits, and details, we prayed for you to deeply experience His unfailing love, indescribable peace, and pure joy. It is our sincere hope that through these Truth-filled pages your heart will be blessed, knowing that God cares about you—your desires and disappointments, your challenges and dreams.

*He knows. He cares. He loves you unconditionally.*

**BLESSINGS!**
**THE DAYSPRING BOOK TEAM**

---

**Additional copies of this book and**
**other DaySpring titles can be purchased**
**at fine bookstores everywhere.**
**Order online at <u>dayspring.com</u>**
**or**
**by phone at 1-877-751-4347**

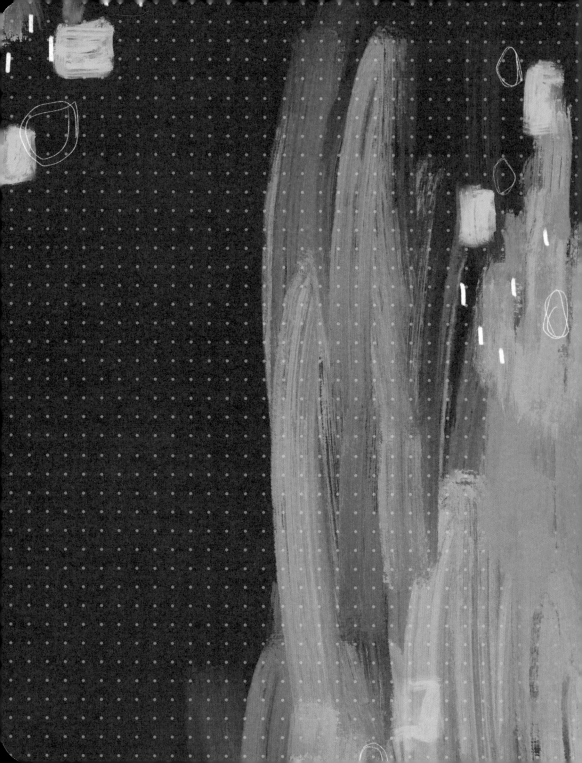